CONFLICT AND COMPROMISE
International Law and World Order
in a Revolutionary Age

CONFLICT AND COMPROMISE
International Law and World Order in a Revolutionary Age

Edward McWhinney

Holmes & Meier Publishers, Inc.
New York

To John N. Hazard

First published in the United States of America 1981 by
HOLMES & MEIER PUBLISHERS, INC.
30 Irving Place, New York, N.Y. 10003
Copyright © 1981 by Edward McWhinney
All rights reserved

Library of Congress Cataloging in Publication Data
McWhinney, Edward.
Conflict and Compromise
Includes index.
1. International Law.   2. International relations.
3. Revolutions.   I. Title.
JX3695.C2M29   1981   341   80-29045
ISBN 0-8419-0694-7
       0-8419-0696-3 (pbk)

Printed in Canada

Design/Maher & Murtagh

Contents

   Acknowledgments / 7
   Foreword / 9
1 Law Among Nations / 13
2 Law and Power / 28
3 The Constitutionalism of World Order / 39
4 The UN Charter: Treaty or Constitution? / 53
5 The Road to Détente / 71
6 Taming the Nations / 80
7 From Peaceful Coexistence to Active International Cooperation? / 95
8 The "Winds of Change" in the World Community / 112
9 A New, Pluralistic, World Law and World Order System / 137
   Table of Cases / 155
   Selected Bibliography / 156
   Index / 159

By the same author

Books (as author)
  Judicial Review in the English-Speaking World (1st ed., 1956; 4th ed., 1969)
  Föderalismus und Bundesverfassungsrecht (1962)
  Constitutionalism in Germany and the Federal Constitutional Court (1962)
  Comparative Federalism. States' Rights and National Power (1st ed., 1962; 2nd ed., 1965)
  "Peaceful Coexistence" and Soviet-Western International Law (1964)
  Federal Constitution-Making for a Multi-National World (1966)
  International Law and World Revolution (1967)
  Conflit idéologique et Ordre public mondial (1970)
  The Illegal Diversion of Aircraft and International Law (1975)
  The International Law of Détente. Arms Control, European Security, and East-West Cooperation (1978)
  The World Court and the Contemporary International Law-Making Process (1979)
  Quebec and the Constitution: 1960-1978 (1979)

Books (as editor)
  Canadian Jurisprudence: The Civil Law and Common Law in Canada (1958)
  Law, Foreign Policy, and the East-West Détente (1964)
  Esquema de un Curso Basico de Derecho Internacional Publico, with F. Cuevas Cancino, et al. (1964)
  The Freedom of the Air, with M.A. Bradley (1968)
  New Frontiers in Space Law, with M.A. Bradley (1969)
  The International Law of Communications (1970)
  Aerial Piracy and International Law (1971)
  Federalism and Supreme Courts and the Integration of Legal Systems, with Pierre Pescatore (1973)
  Municipal Government in a New Canadian Federal System (1980)

Reports (as Royal Commissioner, Commission of Inquiry)
  La situation de la langue française au Québec, 3 vols., with J.-D. Gendron, et al. (1973)
  Parliamentary Privilege and the Publication and Radio and Television Broadcasting of Parliamentary Debates (1974)
  Government Review Commission, City of Vancouver. Report, with R.D. Bell, et al. (1979)

Acknowledgments

Some of the propositions advanced in the present volume were tested, as experimental hypotheses, in lectures to the Centro de Relaciones Internacionales of the Facultad de Ciencias Politicas y Sociales of the Universidad Nacional Autónoma de México in Mexico City in May 1978. They were canvassed again, more recently, in seminars and discussions held in the spring of 1980, with faculty and members of the Institute of Law of the Chinese Academy of Social Sciences in Peking, the Department of Law of the Peking University, the East China Institute of Law and Political Science in Shanghai, and the Department of International Politics of the Fudan University in Shanghai. Acknowledgment must also be gratefully made of the opportunity to talk at length with senior officials of the Department of International Organization, Treaties, and Laws, of the Ministry of Foreign Affairs in Peking.
    There are some extra problems and some extra intellectual advantages in trying to communicate one's particular, specialist, scientific discipline either to a highly literate but lay (non-specialist or else broadly interdisciplinary) audience in one's own cultural community, or to a group of specialists in one's own field but from a different culture, particularly if it be a third world culture. One finds, quickly enough, that what one thought of as eternal verities of international law and world public order in general are often no more than particular responses by one's own cultural community to particular social or economic problems of the world community at particular stages in its historical development. Far from being timeless absolutes in themselves, the principles or norms advanced may be rooted in their own space-time dimension, and therefore subject to critical scrutiny and re-examination in the light of new societal facts and new demands and expectations in the world community at large. There is, in fact, nothing like the intellectual challenge of having to defend, on a rigorously scientific basis, a proposition that

one may have been tempted, from one's special cultural and disciplinary background, to consider self-evident.

The new, transcultural, eclectic approach to international law and to world public order in general should permit us to establish a much-needed new balance between law and politics in the world community today. It should also allow us to separate what, in the congeries of existing rules and ordering principles of world public order, is purely relative and therefore subject to revision in the dry light of reason on the basis of a new, more genuinely equitable and inclusive (in transcultural terms) balance of competing societal interests; and what, by contrast, is of more general social utility, transcending its limited historical origins and therefore more likely to serve the interests of that larger and much more representative world community that has developed since the achievement of decolonization, independence, and self-determination on a worldwide scale.

Foreword

From Cold War, to Détente, to Dissonance and Pluralism

The roots of the present study go back to a group of seven public lectures given over the nation-wide radio network of the Canadian Broadcasting Corporation in 1966-67, and published in monograph form under the title *International Law and World Revolution*. The immediate political context of those lectures was the imminent end of the cold war era with the successful inauguration of the de-Stalinization programme within the Soviet Union and the opening up of direct, bilateral negotiation and exchange between the two great political-military blocs — Soviet and Western — that had dominated international relations since the conclusion of military operations in Europe in May 1945. Détente (although the term was, at that time, being used only by the ever-prescient President de Gaulle of France) was being achieved in a series of concrete measures between the two bloc leaders, the Soviet Union and the United States, using essentially pragmatic, empirical, step-by-step methods that were related, at all times, to mutuality of interests or reciprocal give-and-take between the two sides. The progressive unfolding of détente was obscured, for some commentators and political leaders, by the noisy, frequently polemical debate between the Soviet Union and the United States over what Soviet jurists called the international law of peaceful coexistence, and what some Western jurists viewed as a Trojan horse designed to lull the West into a false sense of security while Soviet leaders proceeded, quietly, to plan world domination.

Looking back on that earlier era of transition from cold war to détente, with all the advantages of retrospective wisdom, it is difficult not to be amused by the remnants of cold war rhetoric that one finds in some of the scientific-legal analysis and criticism on both sides of the political-ideological conflict. By 1970, peaceful coexistence had finally become legitimated within the United Nations framework by its codification and adoption in a UN General Assembly resolution, albeit under the Western-favoured euphemism of "friendly relations and cooperation among states." In May 1972, President Nixon and Secretary Brezhnev formally inaugurated an era of détente that had been developing and, in fact, operational for some years, by formally signing a group of Moscow Accords. These included, among their more important agreements, the Anti-Ballistic Missile Systems Treaty and the Interim Agreement on Strategic Offensive Arms.

No sooner had détente become officially established as the basic premise of international law and relations of the post-cold war era than the seeds of decay, within the world public order system that it embodied and implied, became apparent. The United States, the Western bloc leader, was racked with internal dissension in the wake of the civil disobedience campaigns directed against the American military campaign in Vietnam and the strong, interventionist foreign policy bound up with American military involvement in South East Asia. The traumatic shock of the "Watergate" crisis, and the abortive impeachment campaign that nevertheless forced the resignation of President Nixon and indicted the activist, "imperial" presidency and foreign policy practised by virtually all American leaders since President Franklin Roosevelt, contributed to a weakening of the American commitment to military ventures overseas, even in the name of the collective security arrangements to which the United States was committed by treaty. At the same time these events produced increasing uncertainty among the United States' allies over the reliability of American foreign policy commitments abroad and over the American will to lead the great political-military alliance of Western powers that had so characterized the post-World War II era. The resulting factionalism within the Western bloc was balanced by a growing disaffection within the Soviet bloc, the Warsaw Pact countries of Eastern Europe, that was hardly contained by either repressive, governmental, police measures or direct, military intervention such as the Soviet Union's incursion into Czechoslovakia in August 1968. An aging, conservative, Soviet decision-making group seemed incapable either of adjusting gracefully to the stirrings of political pluralism within its own bloc, or of profiting with élan and imagination from evident dissonance within the rival Western bloc.

FOREWORD

Paralleling the internal troubles of the two great political-military blocs and their leaders — more paradoxical because occurring when the cause of big power détente had achieved its apogee, and when the two rival blocs had essentially achieved political-legal accommodation on both the process and the main substantive issues of their past conflicts — were startling new developments in the world community at large. The political consummation of the "new" international law principle of de-colonization and independence — in itself, a more concrete and urgent application of the nineteenth-century liberal principle of national self-determination — meant a very much larger world community than the narrower, post-World War II community that had been so largely congruent with the membership of the two rival blocs. Decolonization, independence, and self-determination, applied in conjunction with other "new" international law principles — national control of national economic resources, and the quest for an overarching, more genuinely democratic, new international economic order — meant that the new participants in the international legal process increasingly resisted the blandishments of the two big powers to rally around either bloc. The third world countries developed as an autonomous political force in their own right, independent of the two great political-military blocs. In the quest for their own distinctive arenas for political expression and political-legal interaction, the third world countries began increasingly to choose the United Nations and its specialized agencies as their forum, because of its relative openness and freedom from big power pressures. The admittance of the People's Republic of China to full membership in the United Nations in 1971 highlighted and also accelerated this movement. We can thus see, at the same time, a de-emphasis of the rôle of the two big powers in the international law-making process as a whole, and a return to the original intention of the UN Charter, to make the United Nations organization the focal point of international organization and of the world public order system.

1 LAW AMONG NATIONS

The "Old" and the "New"

It is a commonplace, by now, to say that we live in a revolutionary age. In a sense, of course, the whole of recorded history has been a process of revolution or at least of change, for in no one era has mankind stood completely still. Even the mediaeval "Dark Ages" contained within them the seeds of the Renaissance and Reformation.

What characterizes the present era, however, and differentiates it sharply from earlier periods of historical development, is the very range and intensity of the changes, and the fact that they are occurring on so many fronts. One has, in this regard, to accept the fact that we are dealing with a world revolution that is really a series of continuing revolutions, finding outlets in numbers of different, if complementary, ways.

The first great revolution of our time, completing a process begun with the outbreak of World War I in 1914 and the subsequent downfall of the old dynasties and empires of Central and Eastern Europe, is what Marxist legal scholars like to identify as the "downfall of imperialism." This began, of course, with the October Revolution of 1917 and the overthrow of the old czarist régime in Russia, and was followed up, after the Central Powers' military defeat in 1918, with the abdications of the Sultan of Turkey, the Emperor of Austria-Hungary, and the German Kaiser. More important than the essentially symbolic replacement of a sultan or emperor by a republican president, were the political changes effected by World War I in the name of nationalism, independence, and liberalism. In deference to Woodrow Wilson's Fourteen Points, the economically viable and politically stable (if unimaginative) dual monarchy of the Habsburgs was replaced by a group of weak and struggling, mutually intransigent "succession states" whose political difficulties were often gravely complicated by racial and religious minority problems and by territorial boundaries that often sacrificed ethno-cultural justice to supposed geopolitical "natural frontiers."

We will return later to the political legacies of the Carthaginian peace imposed on Europe by the victors in a war that was supposed, in one of Woodrow Wilson's inspired phrases, "to end all wars." Suffice it to say, at this point, that Woodrow Wilson's proclaimed ideal of national self-determination reached its ultimate consummation after World War II with the emergence of movements for decolonization, independence, and self-government on a well-nigh universal scale. In some cases self-government was established gracefully by an act of wise statesmanship with an eye to the future, as with the granting of independence to the Indian subcontinent in 1946 by British Prime Minister Attlee's Labour Government. In other cases it was conceded reluctantly and only after an extended test of arms, as with the French recognition of Indo-China under the Geneva Accords of 1954 in the wake of the Dienbienphu military disaster, or the equally belated French acknowledgment of Algerian independence, or the Portuguese government's protracted military resistance to the "national liberation movements" in its ancient colonies in Africa (but not in India, where the Indian government successfully reclaimed the so-called Portuguese enclaves by a unilateral *coup de main*).

However achieved, decolonization has been the most striking historical development of the decades following World War II. The resulting flood of "new" countries — from Africa, Asia, and the Caribbean — has not merely transformed organizations like the United Nations, which rested on an original, if short-lived, "victors' consensus" from World War II; it has created a vast new arena for the competition and interaction of different social and economic systems. It has also brought, in its wake, a whole new range of post-decolonization problems.

With the liquidation of Portugal's colonial empire by the end of the 1970s, the achievement of independence for Angola and Mozambique by force of arms, and the transformation of the white-minority-governed, breakaway British colony of Rhodesia into black-majority-governed, sovereign Zimbabwe in the spring of 1980, classical colonialism — interpreted in United Nations' parlance and in actual political practice as "salt-water imperialism" and the governance of an Asian or African territory by a "parent" European régime — has finally come to an end. Southern Africa (the white-minority-governed Republic of

South Africa) perhaps stands as the lone exception. Does this mean that national self-determination, with which decolonization was always twinned during the 1950s, 1960s, and 1970s as an imperative principle of international law, has also been achieved and that nothing remains to be done under its *aegis*? The question is important not merely for the ethno-cultural minority or regionally-based separatist movements that one finds in so many parts of the non-colonial world today — in Great Britain, France, Belgium, Switzerland, Italy, Spain, and Yugoslavia, for example — but also within the former colonial territories themselves. In the case of the non-colonial countries already referred to, national unity and national sovereignty have been invoked by central governments that have, at the same time, tried to respond to the centrifugal forces within their states by emphasizing constitutional-governmental pluralism and the devolution of key community decision-making power on a federal or generally regional basis. Within the former colonial territories, and in spite of the frequent arbitrariness of political frontiers inherited from the "parent" power, claims by ethnic minorities for national self-determination (or for their union in an ethnically more homogeneous and rational unit with similar ethnic minorities outside the state) have been resisted, by armed force where necessary, in the name of national sovereignty and the integrity of the post-independence territorial frontiers. The principle of legitimacy — a conservative principle at all times — has been invoked to sanctify the political settlement and frontiers inherited from the original colonial powers, lest deference to the more radical, natural-law-based claims to national self-determination destabilize the political situation in post-decolonization Asia and Africa and lead to interminable territorial wars among the "succession" states, on the pattern of post-Westphalia Europe of the seventeenth and eighteenth centuries.

The second great revolution of our time is an ideological one. It began, by most accounts, with the Russian Revolution of 1917 and reached a climax with the cold war conflict of the late 1940s and the 1950s. After 1959 it seemed to take a new turn, with the developing Russian-Chinese schism. World War I, again in conventional Marxist terms, represented the "last working out of the bourgeois-capitalist system" — supposedly its dying gasp. Of course, the Western-based liberal capitalist system survived that conflict, though it underwent profound internal modification as a result of the world economic depression of the late 1920s and early 1930s, and the progressive acceptance — in all major Western democratic societies and eventually by all major political parties — of collectivist, "welfare state" ideals of human dignity and social betterment, and of the community planning techniques that those ideals implied.

When the Iron Curtain finally descended across Central Europe in the late 1940s — thus concretizing, as an effective political reality, the *de facto* settlements resulting from the German military defeat of 1945 and the Russian military occupation of the Balkans, Eastern Europe, and East Germany (including East Berlin) — and the two rival military blocs faced each other across the ideological frontier, they were each rather different from the theoreticians' abstract models of the 1917 vintage. The West, if it ever had been bourgeois-capitalist in the full Marxist sense, had long since evolved into the accepted patterns of the contemporary, social democratic, planned state. The Soviet Union, for its own part, had moved from its original post-1917 idealistic revolutionary fervour, through the modified capitalistic, NEP revival of the early and middle 1920s, on through Stalin's early era of bureaucratic consolidation, the first of the Five Year Plans, the Stalinist Terror of the middle and late 1930s and the great intra-Party purges of the treason trials, and finally to the undisguised authoritarianism of the dictator's last, paranoiac years, which ended with his death in 1953.

We shall have more to say, at a later stage, about the concept of bipolarity and about the twin military bloc system — represented in Europe by the rival, though militarily complementary, NATO and Warsaw Pact systems — that provided the political balance of power or (in a nuclear age) balance of terror on which world peace rested, however delicately and precariously, from the break-up of the victorious World War II Alliance, very shortly after World War II, until the achievement of the Kennedy-Khrushchev détente with the peaceful resolution of the Cuban missile crisis in October 1962. Suffice it to say, for the moment, that bipolarity and the twin military bloc system, projected on a world scale, meant not only a consolidation of political authority within each bloc (including the completion of Soviet political-military hegemony in Eastern Europe by the end of the 1940s), but also a naked struggle for the extension of power beyond the post-1945, tacitly accepted spheres of control and influence. This meant not only incessant probing in borderline areas between the two blocs, where the lines of demarcation had not been clearly drawn (as in Berlin), not only mischief making in "buffer state" areas where internal weakness and uncertainty of purpose seemed to invite a "fishing expedition" (as in Korea), but also continuing propaganda, infiltration, and internal subversion in so-called uncommitted countries in Asia, Africa, and Latin America. As the "winds of change" brought either decolonization or widespread social unrest, these continents tended to become further battlegrounds for the two opposing blocs — battlegrounds where, if direct military action was excluded by tacit agreement, every form of political-psychological pressure, propaganda, and economic blandishment was positively included. This was the competition of the ideologies, designed to demonstrate beyond doubt which system could most quickly and effectively advance a developing or "new" country through the early stages of political nationhood and economic growth to full social and economic well-being.

At this point, we approach the third great revolution of our time. The revolution in economic science and technique has radically transformed the contemporary world community. In one manifestation, the economic revolution may be viewed as an aspect of the decolonization and liberation of former colonial countries that were tied too narrowly, and certainly too exclusively, to the economic fortunes of the parent country. But beyond this, the economic revolution contended that if the lessons of Keynesian economics and of development economics in general are properly applied, a "new" Afro-Asian country need not be condemned by any inexorable laws of economic development to repeat the slow, laboured history of Western states from feudal times before attaining the level of these advanced industrial civilizations. The revolution in economic thought preached that, given the proper initial development aid in terms of both material resources and skilled technical advice, it is possible to progress quickly through the various stages of economic growth and, in some cases, to skip certain stages altogether.

The revolution in economic thought left open the question of which path to the advanced industrial society is the most effective in terms of getting there most quickly and also, perhaps (though this is a highly sophisticated type of inquiry, more likely to be applied in older or declining societies than in the more impatient "new" countries) in terms of minimizing the harm inflicted upon major community values such as free speech, respect for minority rights, and the like. In a sense the answer to this question, involving in part the decision about where to strike the balance between the interests in rapid economic growth and other community values, will determine which of the current three main roads to national development and community well-being — Western liberal capitalist, post-Stalin Soviet Communist, or Chinese Communist — one will opt for.

Nor has the revolution in economic thought, so far, been able to show what to do in a world community where — given that the lessons of progression through the various stages of economic growth have been satisfactorily mastered — the gap in basic standards of living between the present, advanced industrial societies (both Western capitalist and European communist) and the presently developing countries (Asian, African, Caribbean, and Latin American) is continually widening because of the former's more quickly accelerating rate of economic growth. In some respects this ever-widening "margin of misery," cutting across conventional East-West, communist-capitalist alignments and in effect establishing a new North-South alignment in which the economically prosperous confront the economically underprivileged, non-white, vast majority of the world's population, is likely to be the politically most explosive element in the world community for the last part of the century.

The very real frustration of third world political leaders is manifested in their concerted attempt — particularly in the specialized arena of the United Nations General Assembly, where the sheer weight of the "new" countries' voting power has effectively displaced the big power hegemony of yesteryear — to establish a more equitable and inclusive new international economic order by the legislative *fiat* of General Assembly resolutions. Two resolutions were adopted, without vote, by the General Assembly at its sixth special session on 1 May 1974: the Declaration on the Establishment of a New International Economic Order, and the related Programme of Action on the Establishment of a New International Economic Order. The further Charter of Economic Rights and Duties of States was adopted by the General Assembly at its twenty-ninth regular session on 12 December 1974 (this time by a recorded vote of 120 to 6, with 10 abstentions). Taken together these clearly constitute a code of imperative principles of the "new" international law — here, the new international economic law. But the gap between abstract law-in-books and community "living law" (or law-in-action) is nowhere more apparent than in this area. For it is clear that, under the present international economic system, the active cooperation and assistance of the first and second world ("have") countries, both liberal capitalist and communist, will be needed to translate these postulated ideals of the third world ("have not") countries into concrete, operational terms in the world community today. Unless there is some change in the basic, intellectual attitudes of first and second world countries, substantive changes in the world economic order must be accompanied or even preceded by substantive changes in power alignments in the world public order system itself. In this regard, Mohammed Bedjaoui, one of the most distinguished members of the "new wave" of third world jurists, seems right to insist on linking the quest for a new international economic order with the more general obligation of our times to devise a "new" or "renewed" international law.

The last main revolution in the present era of continuing world revolution is the revolution in science and technology. In its most dramatic form, this is represented by the advent of the nuclear age and the development of large-scale nuclear weapon technology, which has transformed conventional warfare and introduced an uneasy, big-power nuclear "balance of terror" on which world peace now rests. The spread of nuclear science and technology has, however, introduced the dangers of wide-spread proliferation of nuclear weapons and nuclear irresponsibility on the part of a host of medium-sized or smaller countries, in place of the nuclear détente (or tacit understandings as to non-user of nuclear weapons) arrived at by the "responsible" nuclear powers — especially the two bloc leaders, the Soviet Union and the United States. This development, and the progressive weakening of internal control within each of the two main political-military blocs as Soviet-Western détente has been extended and the danger of a direct confrontation between the two bloc leaders largely disposed of, have introduced a new element of instability into international relations that creates an urgent need for new and more comprehensive rules and patterns of world public order.

Beyond this, of course, the onset of the space age, with the massive scientific advances of the post-World War II years, has opened up exciting new challenges that seem to demand scientific collaboration in joint programmes transcending ideological frontiers rather than the isolation that has seen the best scientific manpower in each ideological system forced to work in the watertight compartments established by political boundaries. The space age, even more than the nuclear age, seems to offer the dramatic possibility of an international law of positive cooperation in place of the old international law of conflict.

Impressive cooperation in space research and exploration was achieved between the Soviet Union and the United States in the latter years of the Johnson administration and, especially, during the Nixon administration after the detailed Moscow Summit Accords of May 1972. This was highlighted, in the space area, by the Soviet-US Agreement concerning Cooperation in the Exploration and Use of Outer Space for Peaceful Purposes of 24 May 1972, which was both a logical successor to and a building upon the general idea of the peaceful uses of outer space embodied in the jointly (Soviet and US) sponsored, general Treaty on Principles Governing the Activities of States in the Exploration and Use of Outer Space, Including the Moon and other Celestial Bodies, of 27 January 1967. Unfortunately, the momentum of Soviet-US space cooperation was lost in the late 1970s, as one of the casualties of the revived Soviet-US tensions that marked the end of the Carter administration's four-year term.

In the related area of international communications — and specifically international telecommunications by satellites and satellite television broadcasting — the opportunity for fruitful Soviet-US collaboration was passed by in the mid-1960s when the relevant international organizational infrastructure was being established, probably because of the implications for cold war ideological competition and the continuing propaganda war between the two blocs. Instead, two separate and rival international organizations were established — the US-dominated INTELSAT and the Soviet bloc INTERSPUTNIK. As a result, the establishment of minimum international ground rules to control programme content that approaches the level of propaganda deliberately beamed to rival bloc countries, and to prevent accidental spillover of one country's programmes into another country's receivers without its prior permission, has been left to general accords devised on the basis of difficult, *ad hoc* bilateral negotiation between the two rival blocs. This is a pity. As an entirely new area of activity, without the historical backlog of cold war hostilities, international communications — like general space research and exploration — had seemed to offer the prospect of developing its own autonomous corpus of legal principles and its own distinctive international administrative organization in direct response to its special technological imperatives.

We have spoken to date of the revolution in the world community — in the society in which international law or any framework and basic patterns of world public order must operate. And the question must now be asked, Has there been a corresponding revolution in international law and juridical concepts of world public order? For we teach, in our national law schools, of the necessary relation or symbiosis between law and society — between positive law rules and written prescriptions, and the community in which those same rules are to operate. For without a certain minimum correspondence between the positive law and basic societal facts, the positive law is doomed to remain law-in-books — mere hortatory propositions that will never become community "living law." There was a time — particularly between the two world wars — when national political leaders indulged light-heartedly and incontinently in the poetry of international law-making, and regarded their work as complete when they had elaborated an ideal code at an appropriately high level of generality and abstraction. The 1928 Kellogg-Briand Pact to "outlaw war" is a perfect example of just such a casual act of international legislation by simple fiat, without much concern for the tiresome, underlying causal factors of international tension whose removal or alleviation could alone give meaning to the law makers' high-level declaration and help make it genuine international law-in-action. For in its own historical context of continental Europe and the West between the two world wars, the Kellogg-Briand Pact skated easily over the underlying causes of international tensions at that time. The essentially one-sided Peace Treaty of Versailles of 1919 had placed all political and moral responsibility for the First World War — a classic example of a war of colliding imperial systems — on the defeated Central Powers. It had also imposed the full burdens of ignominious foreign military occupation, forced territorial transfers, and crippling economic reparation on those who had so narrowly lost the War. The Carthaginian Peace of 1919 inevitably contained within itself the seeds of its own decay (as even the victors lost faith in its inherent rectitude and political common sense), and the seeds of its eventual challenge (again by traditional means — recourse to armed force).

Today we are much more pragmatic and empirical in our approach to international problem solving, and less inclined to believe that absolutist solutions involving the destruction of a defeated enemy or the elimination of an ideological opponent can produce lasting solutions. The aftermath of World War II, when the leaders of the victorious coalition competed with each other in political and economic offers to the defeated enemies, Germany and Japan, on whom they had imposed full guilt for the War and also unconditional surrender only several years before, should induce a new element of modesty as well as freedom from hypocrisy and the temptation to preach one's own highly subjective, too often completely self-serving, version of morality, in the practical conduct of foreign policy. We teach, in any case, that exercises in abstract, high-level postulation of *a priori* principles, without first studying the underlying problems to which such principles are supposed to relate and indeed to provide a solution, are exercises in political and legal irresponsibility. They are the more reckless and uncaring because their political authors too often know in advance that the high hopes they engender are likely to end in cruel deception.

If we look at the corpus of "classical" or traditional international law today, we find that, on its surface and as practised by its main interpreters and appliers — *honoratiores* or "dignitaries" of the law, as the great German sociologist Max Weber called them — it displays little that might be called revolutionary. This takes us back to the origins of classical international law itself, and the concept of the international society whose needs and aspirations it was supposed to represent.

It is not so very long since the international society of effective participants in international relations among states (what we today, in the spirit of universalism, call the world community) was considered limited to the "civilized nations," these being the Western European or European-derived, essentially Christian societies that had been founded on the rise of commerce. The fiction was that these countries found their legal personality in their juridical sovereigns and that international law was the expression of their collective conscience. Deference to international law and acceptance of its binding force was effectuated through the principle of comity, and the notion of the ethical obligation of each head of state, as a Christian monarch, to give effect to agreements or to commonly observed, customary rules of conduct. By the beginning of the nineteenth century, the membership of the world community had been expanded, by common consent, to take in a non-Christian society, Turkey. And in the latter half of the nineteenth century, coinciding with the new era of modernization and Westernization inaugurated by Emperor Meiji after 1867, the bounds of the world community were stretched to encompass Japan. All others — nation-states, private associations, or individuals — while capable of being objects of international law and bound by its obligations, were not subjects of international law, who were entitled to claim the benefit of rights deriving from it.

The character and content of classical international law, right down to the present day, reflects the ideological narrowness and cultural homogeneity of the original "family compact." For classical international law is not merely rooted in Western legal writings, court decisions, and state practice; its substantive content tends to reflect the interests being pressed by the politically dominant Western societies during the heyday of their commercial and industrial expansion abroad.

Some of these rules, it must be said, may claim a more general acceptance today based on an asserted reasonableness and common sense that transcends their particular conditions of origin. This was thought to be the case with the classical law of the sea which, as first developed by the early seventeenth-century Dutch writer Hugo Grotius, recognized the common interests in free commercial navigation unrestricted by too many or overly pressing claims of national sovereignty. National sovereignty was essentially limited, at least until the recent Geneva Conferences on the law of the sea, to a three-mile territorial sea. This concept prevailed over the early Portuguese and Spanish claims to national paramountcy even on the high seas. Yet after remaining largely unchallenged for three hundred years, the classical international rules making up the law of the sea began to crumble before the drive of so many states for national appropriation of the wealth of the sea, the continental shelf, and even the deep ocean floor.

The pressure for change came from the third world states (logically, and perhaps with a certain moral claim of right) but also from first and second world countries. President Truman's 1945 proclamation of the United States' sovereignty over the continental shelf adjacent to the American coast — a unilateral act directed immediately towards national appropriation of offshore oil deposits — opened the floodgates to other countries. As the French jurist René-Jean Dupuy concluded, the law of the sea, which according to classical doctrine had essentially been a law of movement, became transformed into a law of appropriation, with the accent shifting from a personal law to a territorial law characterized by a new parochialism in place of the old universalism. In fact, the law of the sea has become an integral part of the law on the new international economic order — one important means of redressing the current imbalance between third world countries and privileged, post-industrial societies.

The three-mile territorial sea disappeared before these concerted national demands. Only the great military-naval powers (the Soviet Union and the United States), or countries like Japan without either a perceptible continental shelf or fishing resources close to their coasts, or the unfortunate landlocked states, were interested in resisting pressures to change the old rules. It is, of course, among the ironies of our time that not all third world countries, because of the accidents of geography, were capable of effectively sharing in that part of the new international economic order now annexed to a redefined, updated law of the sea, and that some of the wealthiest postindustrial societies — the United States and Canada, for example — are among its principal economic beneficiaries.

That part of the law of war known as *temperamenta belli* and devoted to mitigation of the barbarities and cruelties of warfare was also a concept first sponsored by Grotius, in reaction to the senseless outrages and gratuitous violence of the Thirty Years War. It might seem to correspond so obviously to general world community interest today as to need no justification. And yet the development of new modes of armed conflict — the "wars of national liberation" mounted by irregular, "rebel" or guerrilla forces against the parent European colonial power or, as in Vietnam, against the US Army and its "client" government — has called the traditional rules into question where they limit their protection to regular members of the regular armed forces of a recognized government engaging in declared war. For that matter, it is asserted, the rebel or guerrilla forces may not merely claim the full privileges of the law of war for their actions against the colonial power; there may even be an affirmative duty cast upon other states to help such rebel forces in their armed struggle for decolonization and independence.

The narrowness of the original ideological basis of international law is evident. It is the legacy of the historical accident that the original *honoratiores* who largely created its main substantive rules and principles were Western European and Christian. As the respected *Instituto Interamericano de Estudios Juridicos Internationales* declared, in a group study prepared in 1964:

> The continuing political and territorial expansion that the European powers so often achieved through military means brought with it and left in its wake a large number of myths. Perhaps the most significant of these was the concept of the inherent universality and perennial nature of international law — a concept that was linked with the old and undefined concepts of natural law. A derivative belief was that *a priori* juridical standards, which could be demonstrated and justified by pure reason and which politically antedated European territorial expansion, governed juridical relations among states . . . . The immanence of a state order

was assumed and propositions which historically seemed very closely correlated to the political self-interest of the European powers were accepted as juridical norms.

By their talents and vigour the European peoples extended their influence throughout the world; and Westernization almost came to be considered as an essential requisite to the achievement of progress. Meanwhile the myth of the immanence and immutability of international law remained unchanged. Even those authors who made studies of the history of international relations *before* the political predominance of the West tended to acknowledge Western Christian standards as the apex of the development of international juridical norms.

The two world wars of this century dispelled these assumptions. The framework of the world changed, and for the modern state the classical international machinery was no longer sufficient. . . . Wars were no longer investments in blood and steel made by states to round out their borders or to acquire markets. They were sudden blazes of destruction and hatred which swept away the juridical order — improperly observed, but at least existent — that limited conflicts. Colonial expansion, which no longer had the characteristics of Victoria's days, is another example. Freedom of trade, the protection of nationals abroad, and the propagation of Christianity ceased to be justifications. Christianity was no longer regarded as the only true religion, and all peoples were thought to have the right to live out their destiny without undergoing Westernization.

The dissatisfaction that so much of the non-Western membership of the contemporary world community now feels with the historically-received, "classical" international law that must be applied to present-day problems, is indicated in varied representative reactions.

Among jurists, the late and gifted Professor Eugene Korovin — the *doyen* of Soviet international lawyers for many years — called in 1961 for the replacement of what he identified as the "routine system" of international law by a new programme that would express the "epoch of struggle between two opposing social systems; the epoch of Socialist revolutions; the collapse of imperialism; the abolition of the colonial system; the transition on to the Socialist road of more and more peoples; and the victory of Socialism and Communism on a world scale."

The representative of one of the "developing" African countries, at the special United Nations Conference on International Law held at Mexico City in the fall of 1964, bitterly attacked the Statute of the World Court for its identification (in Article 38 (1) (c)) of "the general principles of law recognized by civ-

25

ilized nations" — as one of the sources of law that the court is to apply in deciding cases coming before it. This provision, the African representative said, was hardly likely to dispel the "new" countries' general lack of confidence in the World Court.

In the World Court itself, widened intellectual-legal horizons corresponding to marked extensions in membership in the official world community following the influx of Afro-Asian countries to the United Nations from the mid-1950s onwards, and reflecting, for the first time, an effective Afro-Asian voice in the special political constituency (the UN General Assembly and the UN Security Council) charged with the election of judges to the court, show up in the occasional judicial special opinion. Thus Judge Ammoun, in his specially concurring opinion in *North Sea Continental Shelf* in 1969, also took aim at the concept of "the general principles of law recognized by civilized nations" enshrined in Article 38 (1) (c) of the Court Statute:

> The discrimination between civilized nations and uncivilized nations, which was unknown to the founding fathers of international law, the protagonists of a universal law of nations, Vittoria, Suarez, Gentilis, Pufendorf, Vattel, is the legacy of the period, now passed away, of colonialism, and of the time long-past when a limited number of Powers established the rules, of custom or of treaty-law, of a European law applied in relation to the whole community of nations. Maintained and sometimes reinforced at the time of the great historical settlements — Vienna 1815, Berlin 1885, Versailles 1920, Lausanne 1923, Yalta 1945 — European international law had been defended by jurists of indisputable authority in the majority of branches of international law. . . . However great and powerful the thinking of these renowned jurists may be, their concept of a family of European and North Atlantic nations is nonetheless beginning to be blurred by the reality of the universal community, in the thinking of the internationalists of a new age such as S. Krylov, M. Katz, W. Jenks and M. Lachs. What is more, the universalist jurists of Europe had been preceded by those of Asia and the Middle East: Sui Tchoan-Pao, Bandyo-Padhyoy, Rechid. . . .
>
> The criterion of the distinction between civilized nations and those which are allegedly not so has thus been a political criterion — power politics — and anything but an ethical or legal one. The system which it represents has not been without influence on the persistent aloofness of certain new States from the International Court of Justice.

Judge Ammoun returned to this theme in another specially concurring opinion, rendered as part of the World Court's advisory opinion in *Western Sahara* in 1975, when he rejected the European and Western concept of territory as *terra nullius* and therefore legally open to annexation and colonization by imperial powers. The standard applied by the European powers was highly subjective and always self-serving — "the materialistic concept of *terra nullius*, which led to this dismemberment of Africa following the Berlin Conference of 1885," in Judge Ammoun's own words.

An African jurist, Judge Forster, in his specially concurring opinion in the same *Western Sahara* advisory opinion, echoed Judge Ammoun. Judge Forster found that the court's official opinion of court in that case, being rooted in essentially European and Western legal ways of thought, "minimis[ed] the exceptional importance of the geographical, social and temporal contexts of the problem. . . . It is Africa of former times which is in question, as to which it cannot arbitrarily be required that its institutions should be . . . a carbon copy of European institutions."

All this indicates, of course, that there is a fairly widespread crisis of confidence in international law today. For many peoples, particularly in the "new" countries, the corpus of classical, historically-derived international law provides no affirmative base for satisfying their claims for economic advancement and social betterment. In many respects, it seems to represent a positive barrier to those claims. And organizations like the World Court and the United Nations policy-making organs — which, for most of their history, have seemed to many peoples, particularly in the "new" countries, to be essentially Western-composed or Western-dominated — have too often seemed to be more preoccupied with the petit-point of international law than its imaginative reshaping to meet radically new conditions in international society. The prime task of the international lawyer today becomes, therefore, one of building a new system of world public order with an ideological base broad enough to derive support from, and to encompass, all the main competing, social and economic systems of the present day; and of developing, in the international arena, that necessary symbiosis between positive law and social change that we regard as axiomatic for our own internal law system. In a word, any viable system of world public order or international law must capture the dynamic of the world revolution of our time. How this can best be attempted in a world of ideological conflict will be the subject of the succeeding discussion.

2 LAW AND POWER

Competing (Communist and Western) Systems of World Order

In a widely-quoted address to the American Society of International Law in Washington in the spring of 1963, former Secretary of State of the United States Dean Acheson took as his theme the "quarantine" measures applied by the United States administration during the October 1962 Soviet-Western crisis to ensure the removal of Soviet offensive, ground-to-ground, nuclear missiles from Cuba. The quarantine measures, in Dean Acheson's view, were:

> ... not a legal issue or an issue of international law as these terms should be understood. Much of what is called international law is a body of ethical distillation, and one must take care not to confuse this distillation with law. We should not rationalize general legal policy restricting sovereignty from international documents composed for specific purposes. ...
>
> I must conclude that the propriety of the Cuban quarantine is not a legal issue. The power, position and prestige of the United States had been challenged by another state; and law simply does not deal with such questions of ultimate power — power that comes close to the sources of sovereignty. I cannot believe that there are principles of law that say we must accept destruction of our way of life. ... No law can destroy the state creating the law. The survival of states is not a matter of law.

Dean Acheson's remarks served to call attention to the fundamental dilemma of international lawyers of that particular era, and not less of our own: the relation between law and power and the fundamental, political facts-of-life of the world community at any time. Dean Acheson's era was characterized by big power confrontation and interaction, and resultant conflict or cooperation between the two bloc leaders whenever one of them assumed its own special interests to be threatened. The formal legal structure of world order — the law-in-books — may still have been what it was at war's end in 1945, that is, "one world" represented by a United Nations organization in which all states, large or small, were represented and in which all were subject to the one international law. The realities of the international law-in-action, however, were that once the wartime "alliance against fascism" had achieved its original purpose with the final military defeat of the Axis powers, and once the victors had begun to quarrel among themselves over the spoils of victory in Europe and Asia, the original "one world" premise of the United Nations disappeared. Once the Iron Curtain had fallen across Central Europe, as it effectively had within a year of the conclusion of the war, the *de facto* postwar military settlement of 1945 began to be legitimized with the creation of the twin political-military bloc systems, NATO and the Warsaw Pact — each dominated and largely controlled, in the early years, by the respective bloc leaders, the United States and the Soviet Union. The United Nations, whose constitutional structure, at least, had been predicated upon the premise of continuing big power cooperation in the postwar years, found itself transformed into an arena, and not necessarily the most important arena, for big power ideological confrontation and for the struggle for competitive political advantage between the two blocs. In those situations where the two bloc leaders chose to bring their political disputes before the United Nations, the naked power struggle and the continuing pressure for tactical advantage in the Security Council, the General Assembly, and the specialized agencies as an aid to the warfare of the ideologies, transformed the whole character of the United Nations. For, as a body conceived of and brought into being along basically classical, Western-derived, constitutional lines, the United Nations' ability to work usefully, and ultimately to survive as an effective political force, depended upon respect for the parliamentary "rules of the game" and for at least minimal intra-organization cooperation, mutual respect, and decency.

When the two bloc leaders chose *not* to bring their disputes before the United Nations, however (and this became true of an increasing number of major issues), the political by-passing of the United Nations weakened its political authority and inevitably its efficacy as an arena for international problem solving. Beyond this, the recourse to big power direct action, which the by-passing of the United Nations necessarily involved, encouraged the view that power, not law, was the decisive element in international problem solving, and so helped to weaken respect for international law generally in the postwar world community.

To look again at the example taken by Dean Acheson as the theme for his exegesis on the relation between law and power — the Cuban missile crisis of October 1962 — the most striking fact is that, in a big power, face-to-face ("eyeball to eyeball" as Kennedy termed it) confrontation between the two bloc leaders that brought the world to the brink of full-scale nuclear war, all the significant dealings between the two bloc leaders occurred directly, usually in the form of personal exchanges between the two heads of state, President Kennedy and Premier Khrushchev. And the final settlement — the Soviet agreement to withdraw offensive, ground-to-ground missiles from Cuba in return (one understands) for a tacit American undertaking not to invade Cuba or to attempt to overthrow Fidel Castro by direct, military means — was achieved in a series of private messages between the two heads of state. To be sure, at a certain stage during the American "quarantine action" against Cuba, the Organization of American States was brought into the act, but the important fact is that this occurred only after President Kennedy and his advisers had decided upon the naval blockade. To be sure, US Ambassador to the United Nations Adlai Stevenson gave the United Nations advice concerning American actions and attitudes to the Soviet nuclear investment in Cuba at various stages, but Ambassador Stevenson at no time seemed to be influential in US executive decision making during the Cuban missile crisis. His various statements in the UN arena at all times succeeded, and in no way seemed to have preceded or shaped, the actual American decision making.

If we look at the really crucial breakthroughs in international relations in that postwar era, transcending the ideological frontiers on a genuine, inter-systems basis, we tend to find again that they were achieved outside the United Nations arena, and usually on a direct, person-to-person basis between the two bloc leaders. One understands that Premier Khrushchev of the Soviet Union preferred direct, bilateral negotiation with the American head of state for resolving major East-West issues, because of a certain distaste for open, public negotiation, with its frequent noisiness and playing to the gallery that often occurs at the expense of conflict resolution. Premier Khrushchev was a man who understood the facts of power, of course. One of his most famous comments upon the international scene was a rebuke to the Albanian political leaders for their "irresponsible" approach to international relations in the nuclear era. As Premier Khrushchev said:

> To use a familiar expression: "blessed is he who jabbers about war without knowing what he is talking about." The Albanian leaders talk a lot about rocket and nuclear war, but nobody is worried about their talk. Everyone knows that they have nothing to their name but idle talk and that they have no real possibilities. As you see, our positions on these questions and our responsibilities are different.

Premier Khrushchev, a colourful man with a keen tactical sense, was not above using an international forum like the United Nations to score propaganda points. His celebrated shoe-banging episode in the United Nations General Assembly was an example of his bold and imaginative, if somewhat crude, skill in capturing newspaper headlines. But Premier Khrushchev also had a certain feeling for the right time and the right occasion. He recognized, therefore, that one should not confuse an occasion for propaganda-making with an occasion for actual problem solving. When it came to problem solving, his view was that the really serious business of resolving Soviet-Western conflicts should not be obscured, delayed, or defeated by having a whole lot of unnecessary, unimportant or "irresponsible" people around to complicate fundamental bargaining between the two players who alone led from a position of strength and power — the United States and the Soviet Union.

Premier Khrushchev's preferences as to the *method* of resolving fundamental Soviet-Western conflicts seem to have been shared by American political leaders, in the Kennedy years at least, in reaction to the talkativeness and sheer capriciousness of so many state representatives in the greatly expanded UN General Assembly of recent years. As a result of this coincidence of US and Soviet views, the Kennedy-Khrushchev era was characterized by the private summit meeting of the US and Soviet heads of state or their immediate personal confidants, as the ultimate refinement in method for maintaining international peace and for international law-making in general. This was the method employed, after all, for achievement of the Moscow Nuclear Test Ban Treaty of August 1963. It was negotiated, and its actual text worked out and agreed upon, in personal talks between Soviet Foreign Minister Gromyko and President Kennedy's special representative Mr. Harriman (plus Lord Hailsham of the United Kingdom). It is true that UN Secretary-General U Thant was invited to be present at the formal signing of the treaty in Moscow on 8 August 1963, but the invitation seems to have been a polite afterthought; in any case, it did not reflect any actual United Nations contribution to the successful conclusion of the treaty. Likewise, the Nuclear Test Ban Treaty, after its formal signing in Moscow by the three principals who had actually worked it out, was made open to other states for adherence, and in fact more than a hundred states have since signed it. However, these lesser states were powerless to change the text of the treaty and of course in no way had been consulted about, or had contributed to, its final terms.

In measure, one might say the same thing about the 1967 UN-based Treaty on the Peaceful Uses of Outer Space. In contrast to the Moscow Test Ban Treaty, the Space Treaty was, as a formal matter, handled by a special UN Committee, and individual jurists outside the United States and the Soviet Union made important contributions to it (especially Polish jurist and then chairman of the special UN Committee, Manfred Lachs, later elected a Judge of the World Court). Nevertheless, the treaty only became inevitable once — within a day of each other in June 1966, and with a synchronization of timing and drafting that bespeaks months of private bilateral US-Soviet discussions — the US and the Soviet Union submitted substantially identical drafts for a treaty. The final text of the Space Treaty, agreed upon in December 1966, was essentially an assimilation and blending of these two drafts.

Reference to the *method* of resolving international tensions and to the preference of the two bloc leaders, during the heyday of Soviet-US détente in the 1960s and the early and mid-1970s, for by-passing the United Nations in favour of quiet diplomacy *inter partes* and more streamlined, certainly speedier machinery for international problem solving, leads to the issue of the substantive nature of the conflict resolution — meaning, here, the actual law to be applied. The Cuban missile crisis of October 1962, and the rôle of international law in its actual resolution, were the subjects of sustained discussion and debate in North American legal circles. The 1964 Annual Meeting of the American Society of International Law in Washington, for example, was largely built around this theme. From the American viewpoint, the *political* problem in the Cuban crisis of October 1962 — once the Soviet emplacement of offensive, ground-to-ground nuclear weapons in Cuba had been satisfactorily established by aerial overflights, photographic evidence, and intelligence reports — was to remove what President Kennedy's military advisers assured him was a major disturbance to that cold war military "balance of power" (or "balance of terror," in nuclear terms) on which world peace had rested since the break-up of the victorious World War II coalition and the establishment of the Iron Curtain in Central Europe. We know now the gravity of the threat presented to the North American defence system by the clandestine Soviet nuclear incursion into Cuba. For the offensive, ground-to-ground nuclear weapons, directed from military bases in Cuba, would have effectively by-passed the tightly organized "northern approaches" radar defence network. While a similar "southern approaches" radar defence network existed, it had never been given the priority accorded to the northern screen, for the very simple reason that an attack from the south, on Washington or New York, had never figured highly in Western military planners' expectations. The effect of Premier Khrushchev's "fishing expedition" into Cuba — induced, one understands, by the Soviet Chiefs of Staff view that they could create a nuclear fait accompli undetected by American intelligence, and by Premier Khrushchev's own hunch, based on his meeting with President Kennedy in Vienna the year before, that the American President was a weak man who would tolerate even a disturbance of the political-military status quo adverse to American interests rather than risk a nuclear war — would have been to establish a new and massive nuclear threat on America's southern flank, against which no really effective advance warning system existed up to that time (the fall of 1962). Though Premier Khrushchev's official statements, after his Cuban nuclear ploy had been publicly revealed, all asserted that the attempt to place nuclear weapons in Cuba was an essentially friendly, non-aggressive gesture to aid a fraternal, communist country against threats of future invasion by the forces of imperialism (the United States), Premier Khrushchev and his Chiefs of Staff did not limit themselves to defensive, ground-to-air missiles but included substantial numbers of purely offensive, ground-to-ground missiles capable of reaching Washington and New York. This fact exposed the true purpose of the venture as a covert attempt to introduce a new nuclear factor into the existing balance of power. One notes, in this regard, that one of the principal counts in the official Soviet denunciation of Premier Khrushchev on the occasion of his dismissal from office in the fall of 1964 was his alleged nuclear "irresponsibility" in having ventured so abruptly and cavalierly into a recognized American sphere of political influence, thereby threatening the cold war military status quo and provoking the risk of massive American retaliation, and escalation into a full-scale nuclear war.

We have been speaking of the *political* or *political-military* problem presented for the United States and the West by the clandestine Soviet nuclear incursion into Cuba, as a disturbance of the existing cold war balance of power that had, since Stalin's death at least, been tacitly recognized and mutually observed by both the Soviet bloc and the West. There were some people in the United States, perhaps, who wished to characterize the *political* problem more broadly as an ideological threat to American political and economic interests in the Americas — posed not so much by Premier Khrushchev's nuclear infiltration, as by the mere fact of the continued existence of Fidel Castro's Communist régime after the abortive US-sponsored, "Bay of Pigs" insurgent landings in April 1961. To his credit, President Kennedy rejected any such characterization of the Cuban crisis in narrowly anti-Castro, anti-Communist terms. He insisted on viewing it in the context of Soviet-Western relations and the maintenance of the East-West *de facto* political-military balance. This meant limiting the political-military problem, vis-à-vis hemispheric defence, to the new Soviet offensive nuclear presence in the Americas, and limiting the political-military solution to securing the removal of the Soviet offensive nuclear weapons from Cuba. It excluded, on this basis, any attempt by the President to expand the political-military solution to the problem and make the occasion an excuse for getting rid of Fidel Castro and his government, once and for all, by direct military action.

Once he had characterized the political problem and its preferred political solution, with a restraint that did credit to his calmness and prudence of political judgement, President Kennedy was faced with the problem of choosing the *legal* solution — meaning the particular international law machinery and substantive principles to invoke in support of the action to be taken. This is not meant to imply that the political and the legal characterizations were temporally separated in the act of executive decision making in the Cuban crisis, with the choice of legal means and remedies being looked at only *after* all the crucial policy options had been considered and the final choice arrived at on political grounds. There are, it is true, some students of the continental *Realpolitik* school who will always argue that the executive decision maker makes his choices on a basis of naked power and national interest alone, and then calls in his international lawyers to provide polite footnotes for later historians or respectable window-dressing for public opinion in his own or neutral states. Such a cruelly cynical approach leads inevitably to the pre-World War I doctrine of *Kriegsraison* and to a contempt for international law that is captured in the historic phrase of the 1914 Imperial German Chancellor (Bethmann-Hollweg), dismissing the Belgian Neutrality Treaty of 1831 as a "mere scrap of paper." To his credit, President Kennedy never embraced any such doctrine.

Though an historian and not a lawyer by training, President Kennedy nevertheless had a keen feeling for international law and for legal thought-ways in general. And we know that, in the actual process of executive decision making in the Cuban missile crisis, legal considerations entered into discussion and policy planning right from the outset, and helped to shape the final result and the final choice of means for resolving the problem. As Professor Abram Chayes of the Harvard Law School, then Principal Legal Adviser to the State Department, has revealed:

> The confrontation was not in the courtroom and, in a world destructible by man, a legal position was obviously not the sole ingredient of effective action. We were armed, necessarily, with something more substantial than a lawyer's brief. But though it would not have been enough merely to have the law on our side, it is not irrelevant which side the law was on. The effective deployment of force, the appeal for world support, to say nothing of the ultimate judgment of history, all depend in significant degree on the reality and coherence of the case in law for our action.

It is an integral part of the legal process to be concerned with questions of ways and means. And one of the principles that we teach, in our national law schools, is economy in the use of power in aid of legal decisions. Given a choice between several alternative modes of reaching a given legal result, the legally correct course of action is the solution that inflicts the least deprivation on other widely-held community values. In other words, one should opt for more moderate legal controls where the alternatives rely too heavily on naked power or direct military action to achieve their result. It is in this respect, especially, that President Kennedy's final policy decision to resolve the Cuban missile crisis was *legal* in the best sense of contemporary international law. Rejecting the advice of the "hawks" in his National Security Council advisory group, who wanted direct aerial bombing of the Cuban missile bases to eliminate the missiles and their firing installations, he opted for the "quarantine" control device in order to ensure effective removal of the Soviet offensive nuclear missiles from Cuba *but to do no more than that*. President Kennedy thus avoided the twin dangers that direct military action and a substantial public display of force might have presented: a public humiliation and consequent loss of face for Premier Khrushchev, which might have unnecessarily exacerbated Soviet-Western relations; and an irrational Soviet military response in kind, which could have triggered a full-scale nuclear war.

It is significant, in this respect, that after the then Soviet Ambassador to the United Nations, Mr. Zorin, made his initial angry (but shortlived) attack in the United Nations, the legality of American actions in the Cuban missile crisis was never very seriously disputed by the Soviet Union. Premier Khrushchev's own ultimate acceptance of the quarantine was, in Walter Lippmann's words, "rather elegant and nonchalant." One does not find, in Soviet scientific legal writings, contests of intellectual stature or public standing of the basic legality of President Kennedy's actions.

But if the legality of the American actions in the Cuban crisis was not actively contested in *Soviet* legal circles, it was, as already noted, the subject of sustained debate in *American* legal circles. This American discussion and criticism tends to go to a seeming American acquiescence in, and indeed sponsorship of, an effective by-passing of the United Nations and UN regionally-based legal machinery in favour of direct inter-bloc legal dealing; or to a substantial expansion of the old international law category of Pacific Blockade, well beyond the limits that had so far been accepted in custom-based international law; or to an interpretation of legally permissible "self-defence" that goes well beyond the provisions of Article 51 of the United Nations Charter (if it does not contravert that altogether) and which seems to postulate a common-law right of self-defence separate from and antecedent to the UN Charter. In fact, the United States administration decided to rely principally, if not exclusively — in the formal ground for its justification, in international law, of the legality of its Cuban quarantine — upon regionally-based legal arguments (in terms of the UN Charter) that looked to the authorization of the US action by the Council of the Organization of American States. Though the acquiescence in or approval of the US action by the member-states of the Organization of American States was never in doubt, and was in fact overwhelming, there was difficulty in bringing the US quarantine under the *aegis* of the OAS as a "regional" (American hemisphere) security action expressly authorized by Chapter VIII of the United Nations Charter. Either because of the time element, or because the matter was simply overlooked, the OAS Council was not approached in advance of US problem solving, and its approval therefore came only after the event as a sort of *ex post facto* ratification of events over which it had no control, either as to substance or to method. Though none would contest the genuineness of the OAS *imprimatur*, it is no doubt regrettable that, through inadvertence, the forms of etiquette pertaining to that authorization were not fully complied with from the outset.

The debate of the 1960s among American international lawyers over the legal grounds of the Cuban crisis action draws attention to some of the main dilemmas of international law in the world community then and now. As a matter of international law-in-action, United Nations-based law could not be said, at that time or even today, to represent one overarching, paramount body of legal principles covering all possible international problems and providing instant, ready-made solutions. Instead, international law, as law-in-action, is really a congeries of separate systems of international law that sometimes operate in separate spheres, sometimes overlap, and sometimes directly conflict. United Nations law is an important part of that congeries of separate international laws, but only a part. In particular, in the heyday of Soviet-US détente, when the fundamental interests of the two main ideological blocs (and especially of their leaders, the Soviet Union and the United States) clashed, it would have been unrealistic, as a matter of international law-in-action, to expect such vital interests to be resolved in the arena of the United Nations, or to blame the United Nations for having failed to provide a solution. The Western bloc, after the political high-water mark of the "Uniting for Peace Resolution" passed by the UN General Assembly on 3 November 1950, had lost majority control of General Assembly proceedings by the mid-1950s with the large-scale admission of newly decolonized Asian and African third world countries who effectively altered the post-1945 voting balance in the main United Nations organs and, above all, in the General Assembly itself. It would be natural for the United States to turn away from the General Assembly for purposes of international problem solving if alternative arenas and alternative techniques should seem to offer better prospects of success than multilateral diplomacy in a public, parliamentary-style setting. In the early and most creative period of Soviet-US détente, during the early and mid-1960s, the Soviet Union (which had never been able to command a majority in the UN General Assembly and was seemingly well-disposed to settling some of its longstanding differences with the West on a basis of mutuality and reciprocity of interest) was prepared to enter into direct, bilateral negotiations in private meetings. The short-term interest of international lawyers was certainly served by the resolution of great international issues like nuclear disarmament, arms control generally, and the security of territorial frontiers in Central and Eastern Europe by *legal* means, whether in the United Nations itself, in the full spirit of the Charter, or by direct, big power negotiations in Summit Meetings *à deux*. The long-term interest remained, however, trying to persuade the big powers to avoid the caprice and simple chance of these bilateral dealings, however well-intentioned, and persuading them to cooperate in institutionalizing settlement of international disputes by setting up appropriate machinery for conflict-resolution before conflicts actually arose. This implied, ultimately, a return to United Nations Charter principles, using Charter-based arenas and techniques for international problem solving. It is a historical irony that, while the more informal route of direct, big power negotiation as a preliminary to more formalized UN-based, general treaties was largely successful in finally resolving the legal issues of the post-1945 territorial settlement in Europe in the early 1970s, and in settling, throughout the 1960s and until the mid-1970s, the major points of disagreement and rivalry between the two big powers as to nuclear weapons development and the appropriate defensive counters, the revived Soviet-US tensions of the late 1970s have brought, in some measure, a return to United Nations arenas and methods — if reluctantly, and *faute de mieux* as a substitute for mutual trust and reliance on the part of the big powers. Since the UN General Assembly has become, today, the main arena for third world activism on behalf of a new, political and economic public order system, in which third world countries will participate and share more equitably, and on behalf of a "new" international law generally, this convergence of basic interests should imply a revived and extended rôle for the United Nations in the 1980s and thereafter.

3 THE CONSTITUTIONALISM OF WORLD ORDER

UN Security Council and General Assembly as "Parliament of Mankind"

The United Nations organization, as achieved at the San Francisco Conference in 1945, was the creation of the victorious "wartime Alliance against Fascism." By definition, the defeated Axis powers did not participate in its creation; nor did the few remaining neutral countries who outlived the war. These latter, indeed, when they later came to apply for membership, had to run the political gauntlet in meeting the legal criteria for membership established under the Charter. The Soviet jurist, Judge Krylov, in a dissenting opinion in the World Court Advisory Opinion of 1948 on Conditions of Admission of a State to Membership in the United Nations, suggested that Eire was not a "peace-loving" state, as stipulated in Article 4 (1) of the Charter, because it had not taken part in World War II. In Judge Krylov's view, to be peace-loving was no mere passive state of mind, as the terms used in the French text of the Charter — "état pacifique" — might imply. On the contrary, the English text's "peace-loving," the Spanish text's "amantes de la paz," and also the Russian and Chinese texts, had a more active sense, which made "tak(ing) part in World War II alongside the democratic countries" a relevant criterion for admission to membership in the United Nations.

The point is, of course, that the United Nations Charter, originally conceived and drafted as a blueprint of world public order, was the creation of only a part of the world community — the victorious Allies. Even here, the actual drafting was the work of a relatively small group of major powers, with the Soviet

Union being rather negative and defensive from the beginning.

Just why the Soviet Union chose to be less than enthusiastic about the embryonic United Nations organization is not hard to discern. Right from its outset, that earlier experiment in a constitutionalism of world order — the League of Nations — had seemed to Soviet jurists to have a bourgeois-capitalist, imperialist orientation. At best, it was a legal device for preserving, for Lloyd George and the other Western heads of state, the fruits of the Carthaginian peace treaty that they had imposed on defeated Imperial Germany at Versailles; at worst, it was a political instrument for containing and defeating the Soviet Union and other forces of world revolution. From its establishment in 1919 until the Soviet Union finally joined in September 1934, the League of Nations was viewed by Lenin and Stalin as an essentially anti-Soviet coalition. During the Soviet Union's brief membership — from 1934 until the League excluded it in December 1939, following the Red Army's invasion of Finland — the Soviet Union had very little reason to be impressed with the effectiveness, as international law-in-action, of this first major attempt at institutionalizing world order along constitutional lines. For these were the years of the breakdown of collective security, and of the League of Nations' ignominious retreat and weakness in the face of naked Italian aggression in Ethiopia, the Japanese military penetration of China, and Nazi Germany's successive repudiations of detailed provisions of the Versailles Treaty in pursuit of its own *irredentist* claims by military threat or direct military action.

In the case of the United Nations, from its first establishment in 1945 it was clear that the Soviet Union could not hope to command a political majority in it, and so to control its proceedings. By joining, the Soviet Union could at best prevent the United Nations from becoming a hostile, anti-Soviet instrument, as (in the Soviet view) the old League of Nations had effectively become without Russian membership in the period from its founding in 1919 until 1934. But this was not an unimportant political objective, and once the decision to join had been made, the Soviet Union's objectives in the actual drafting sessions for the UN Charter became to secure adequate, institutional guarantees in the Charter itself to protect the Soviet Union against the arbitrary will of political majorities in any of the UN's main organs. This initial "defensive" conception of the United Nations, on the part of the Soviet Union and its main associates, explains some of the internal contradictions in the United Nations' final form, and also the Soviet Union's general, long-range attitudes to the United Nations as an arena for fundamental Soviet-Western ideological competition, at least in the first decade and a half of its existence.

The internal contradictions in the United Nations' constitutional machinery are manifested in the uneasy compromise that it effects between the philosopher's conception of "one world" and a genuine, universal "common law of mankind," and the elemental facts of power of the world community characterized by the political system of bipolarity in the immediate post-World War II era.

The "one world" concept is reflected in the attempt to institutionalize world public order in constitutional terms; in the implicit concept of universality of membership in the new organization, albeit a universality that is legally qualified by the "peace-loving" requirement; in the provision for continuing the World Court as the common tribunal of mankind, albeit with a jurisdiction limited by the voluntary submission of states. Those international lawyers who are also constitutional lawyers will recognize immediately some inherent dangers in the institutionalized projection of a "one world" concept that is rooted in essentially Western-derived, special constitutional concepts. We know enough today of the circumstances in which basic, modern Western constitutional ideas were conceived, to be modest about their chances for survival and growth when exported to essentially non-Western societies — as they have been in such large measure since the War to the "new" countries of Asia and Africa. Western constitutionalism, after all, as (in Judge Learned Hand's words) one of "the last flowers of civilization," may flourish under ideal conditions, but it is crucially dependent for its survival on mutual self-restraint and fairness, and (in Judge Learned Hand's words) on that general "spirit of moderation" that tends to be found only in societies that have already achieved their revolutions and have had time to develop more stable legal values. As an exercise in rationalized constitutionalism, Western style, the United Nations Charter bears a resemblance to American constitutional styling and phrasing that is only partly explained by the use of the American poet Archibald MacLeish — in 1945, a US Assistant Secretary of State specially seconded to the San Francisco Conference — as an adviser on the final draft. It is important, however, to recognize that the UN Security Council and the UN General Assembly, like any other Western influenced constitutional organs, are crucially dependent upon constitutional "rules of the game" for their effectiveness and indeed for their survival as viable political institutions. Persistent obstructionism or sheer wilfulness in the face of the majority can, along the lines of the Irish members' conduct in the pre-World War I British House of Commons or a Southern members' filibuster in the United States Congress, bring a parliamentary body to a standstill and defeat or delay its work. On the other hand, a parliamentary majority that recognizes no limits of prudence and self-restraint vis-à-vis minority rights and interests may become equally guilty of contempt for parliamentary processes and ultimately for constitutional government itself. It has been suggested (in different quarters and usually for different reasons) that both of these conditions have been strongly in evidence in the work of the United Nations Security Council and General Assembly at various times since 1945.

Deference to the facts of power — in 1945, the beginnings of bipolarity in the world community — was actually made in the United Nations Charter. It was reflected in the big power veto that was specially built into the voting rights and procedures in the Security Council and in the practical paramountcy in policy-making powers given to the big-power-dominated Security Council vis-à-vis all other UN organs, especially the General Assembly. As a matter of law-in-books, veto power was accorded to all the big powers of 1945. These were the original, wartime "Big Five": the United States, the Soviet Union, Great Britain, France, and China. As a matter of law-in-action, since the other four (China remaining Nationalist China, even after its retreat from the mainland in 1948) all represented the same ideological base and invariably made common cause on major political issues, the Soviet veto operated in the Security Council to defeat Western-sponsored actions. There is no doubt that, in the early years of the United Nations when Stalin was still alive and cold war battle lines were therefore well drawn, the Soviet veto — many times actually used and many times merely threatened to compel withdrawal of announced actions — operated to defeat decisions desired by the overwhelming bulk of UN membership (in the days before the great Afro-Asian influx into the UN). But the consequent United Nations inaction did correspond, more or less, to the political reality of the immediate postwar years until the time of Stalin's death in 1953: no action disturbing the post-1945, *de facto* political-military settlement in Europe could be taken unilaterally — that is, by the West on the one hand or the Soviet Union on the other — without running the risk of escalation into full-scale conflict. In this context, the law (the big power veto and the actual UN practice under it) simply followed the social facts (bipolarity and the twin military bloc system as the basic power configuration of postwar Europe and of the postwar world generally).

The tacit acceptance by both sides, even during the height of the cold war, of the big power veto and the propriety of its actual exercise whenever a big power felt — however irrationally or unfairly — that its own special interests were threatened, explains the extreme fury with which Stalin and his political advisers greeted, in 1950, what they regarded as a unilateral, Western-promoted violation of the UN constitutional "rules of the game" over the Korean crisis.

On 10 January 1950, the Soviet representative in the Security Council submitted a draft resolution proposing that the Security Council should decide "not to recognize the credentials" of the representative of Nationalist China (then, as now, the Chinese government-in-exile in Taiwan after its military defeat and withdrawal from the mainland), "and to exclude him from the Security Council." After the rejection of this proposal, the Soviet representative walked out of the Security Council, and did not return to it until 1 August 1950 when, under the ordinary system of rotation, the Soviet representative, Mr. Malik, became eligible to be President of the Security Council. In the meantime, however, on 25 June 1950, the Security Council took note of the invasion of South Korean territory by North Korean forces and adopted (in the absence of the Soviet representative) a resolution declaring that the North Korean action constituted a breach of the peace and calling for the withdrawal of the North Korean forces. On 27 June 1950 the Security Council voted to recommend that members of the United Nations furnish assistance to the Republic of Korea, and on 7 July 1950 the Security Council proceeded to establish a unified military command led by the United States.

When the Soviet representative, Mr. Malik, returned to the Security Council in August 1950, he bitterly denounced the action taken by the Security Council in the absence of the Soviet representative. To quote from the Security Council debates on the Korean issue, Mr. Malik charged:

> Taking advantage of the absence from the Security Council of ... two permanent members — the USSR and China [Mr. Malik means, here, Communist China] — and dictating its will in the Council to its military and political allies, the United States has hurriedly forced upon the Council a series of illegal and indeed scandalous resolutions, designed on the one hand to cover up United States aggression in Korea and, on the other, to promote

to the furthest possible extent the plans for war in Korea and the Far East by involving other States in this war. . . . The resolutions adopted in the Security Council under the dictate of the United States delegation and in violation of the United Nations Charter have no legal force. They were motivated by the desire of the aggressor to cloak and mask his aggression and are in no way directed towards strengthening the cause of peace.

Even stronger invective was reserved by Soviet jurists for the famous "Uniting for Peace" resolution passed by the UN General Assembly on 3 November 1950 by a vote of 52 to 5, with two abstentions. This was when the UN General Assembly laid down the doctrine that the exercise of the veto by a big power in the Security Council should not paralyze the UN or relieve the General Assembly of its power under the UN Charter. The resolution — Resolution 377 A (V) — declares:

> . . . if the Security Council, because of lack of unanimity of the permanent members, fails to exercise its *primary* responsibility for maintenance of international peace and security in any case . . . then the General Assembly shall consider the matter immediately with a view to making appropriate recommendations to Members for collective measures, including in the case of a breach of the peace or act of aggression the use of armed force when necessary, to maintain or restore international peace and security.

In terms of the "Uniting for Peace" resolution, if the General Assembly is not in session when any such threat to the peace, breach of the peace, or act of aggression occurs, then it may meet in an emergency special session within twenty-four hours of a request initiated either by the Security Council on the vote of any seven members, or by a majority of members of the United Nations.

In the debate on the "Uniting for Peace" resolution in the General Assembly, the chief Soviet delegate, the late Andrei Vyshinsky, saw the Resolution (correctly, no doubt) as designed to circumvent the Security Council and its special voting provisions allowing for the big power veto. Mr. Vyshinsky interpreted the resolution (again correctly, no doubt) as an attempt to revise the Charter principles dividing legal competence between the Security Council and the General Assembly, and thereby to weaken the Security Council in its special role as a guardian of big power interests.

Looking back on the Korean crisis of 1950 and the legal measures taken in the United Nations to resolve that conflict

CONSTITUTIONALISM OF WORLD ORDER

in accordance with the Charter's principles, it is clear that there was a certain *ad hoc* quality to the Western tactical legal response. Just after the peaceful resolution of another, but later, Soviet-Western crisis — the Cuban missile crisis of October 1962 — then US Assistant Secretary of State Harlan Cleveland gave some sage advice as to *methods* of problem solving for cold war conflicts:

> If we are to add one more "lesson from flaps we have known" it would be this: Watch carefully the precedents you set. You will have to live with the institutions you create. The law you make may be your own.

The Security Council action in the summer of 1950, taken in the absence of the Soviet Union, may have been militarily necessary to avert a North Korean takeover of South Korea. But it violated Soviet conceptions of parliamentary legality, for in Soviet legislative bodies an absence is considered equivalent to a negative vote. It also disturbed some Western jurists, to judge by the debate in Western scientific-legal journals over both its legality in UN Charter terms and its political wisdom. There is little question that the continued absence of the Soviet Union during the crucial Security Council debates and votes on the UN Korean action resulted from a lack of adequate policy coordination between the UN operations division of the Soviet Foreign Ministry and Soviet military planners (something that occurs quite as often in the Soviet Union as in the West), rather than from any Soviet conviction that the Soviet Union's absence *per se* would legally paralyze the Security Council. From the viewpoint of Western legal tacticians, the political-military advantages of Security Council-authorized action in Korea would have to be weighed against the resultant damage, if any, to the UN constitutional "rules of the game" as they were then known and observed by both sides in the cold war struggle.

The "Uniting for Peace" resolution, however, was potentially more damaging to settled expectations concerning the operation of UN organs. In the light of the military action already authorized and taken by the Security Council to resolve the Korean crisis, it may be doubted whether the "Uniting for Peace" resolution did more than serve as an additional legal argument — ex *abundante cautela*, as it were — in case the Western-based legal arguments (that a Soviet absence from the Security Council did not equal a Soviet veto) should fail to jell in the court of world public opinion.

This is why it is instructive to consider Harlan Cleveland's comment that one's own *ad hoc* legal arguments may boomerang and be turned against one. The big power veto in the Security Council is a political and legal protection for the Soviet Union, of course, but it can also be useful to the other big powers. The big power veto and the general predominance of the Security Council vis-à-vis the General Assembly were designed to recognize the hard political reality of the post-1945 world, that the big powers were the "responsible" states on whom the ultimate burden of peace or war would rest. More than one Western jurist in the last several years, responding to a Western perception of arbitrariness, immaturity and "irresponsibility" in the UN General Assembly since the influx of "new" countries from Asia, Africa, and the Caribbean, has had second thoughts about the "Uniting for Peace" resolution and the merits of favouring — despite the intentions of the original draftsmen of the UN Charter — an enlargement of the General Assembly's decision-making-powers at the expense of the Security Council. At the time the "Uniting for Peace" resolution was adopted by the General Assembly — on 3 November 1950 — there was, as the near unanimous vote indicates, a substantial pro-Western majority in the General Assembly. This, of course, has not been true since the mid-1950s. When the first wave of Afro-Asian third world countries began to enter the United Nations at that time, there was a certain unpredictability and even incoherence of voting practice before a new majority coalition could crystallize in the UN General Assembly. A more flexible and imaginative Soviet approach, allowing more scope for independent initiative and pragmatic manoeuvring in the General Assembly, might have enabled the Soviet Union and its associates to ally themselves with, if not indeed to lead, the new third world forces. This might, in turn, have encouraged the Soviet Union to reverse earlier, institutional positions derived from earlier, defensive eras when the Soviet Union believed itself doomed to be outvoted in the UN General Assembly as it had been in the League of Nations. Instead of resting with its, by now, traditional conservatism and favouring the Security Council (with its big power veto) at the expense of the General Assembly, the Soviet Union might have attempted to build a "revolutionary" coalition in the General Assembly under its own banner, and to adopt as its principal legal instrument the erstwhile Western "all power to the General Assembly" legal-institutional position developed in aid of the "Uniting for Peace" resolution of 1950. Fortunately, perhaps, for the West, the institutional conservatism that seems to characterize Soviet foreign policy — the bureaucratic weight of old administrative ideas and practices — proved too strong. Or it may be that Soviet policy makers deliberately took a long view and decided not to seek a temporary, and possibly quite shortlived, Soviet advantage in the newly expanded General Assembly. In its long-range perspective, the Soviet Union viewed participation in international organizations as something of a holding operation while it maximized its interests in more overtly political arenas.

For their part, many Western jurists, and the governments that they represented or advised, examined the actual performance of the UN General Assembly from the mid-1950s onwards and during the awkward transition from a comfortable, pro-Western voting majority to a finally quite stable, generally coherent and predictable, third world majority coalition. They reacted against the alleged "playing to the gallery" and the alleged double standards of many countries (frequently police states), and tended to conclude, perhaps too quickly, that the sober business of international problem solving was really too important to be entrusted to such an erratic and uncertain body. This encouraged Western jurists, at that crucial period of transition, to turn their back on the UN General Assembly as an important East-West arena and opt increasingly for direct, bilateral, Summit Meeting-type negotiations with the Soviet Union and the Soviet bloc generally, outside the United Nations. As a secondary consequence, the "Uniting for Peace" resolution would not be lightly invoked by the Western countries who, as between General Assembly and Security Council, would tend to prefer the comparative safety (because of their own big power veto) of the Security Council for dealing with the really serious issues of peace and war.

In spite of the political potential for a Soviet flirtation — along the adventurist lines sketched by the late Professor Korovin — with the new, third world-based forces of political and legal activism within the General Assembly, the Soviet attitude vis-à-vis the General Assembly tended to remain one of caution and reserve. There is a terminal value, as Dewey has noted, in old legal ideas. In the specific context of the United Nations this intellectual conservatism, even timidity, in developing imaginative new policy constructs in response to radically new societal events has meant a certain inevitable time lag between traditional Soviet international legal doctrine on the one hand, and actual Soviet self-interest and political advantage in concrete problem-situations. Professor Gregory Tunkin, the then

Legal Adviser to the Soviet Foreign Ministry, complained that during the Khrushchev era — when the de-Stalinization campaign was well under way in all aspects of Soviet official life — both academic and professional Soviet international lawyers displayed a "weakness and incompleteness in juridical argumentation and a tendency to slip into the easier path of ready-made political argumentation reinforced by quotations." Dr. Tunkin regarded this condition as producing an "isolation from actual reality, from the foreign policy of the USSR as it is practised.... The writers restrict themselves to the cognitive aspect of the problem and do not aim at formulating proposals that can be employed in the practice of Soviet foreign policy...." Dr. Tunkin concluded his philippic with a strong call for freeing Soviet legal science "from dogmatism, from the use of citations instead of creative thought, from crying Hallelujah and from the isolation from actual reality which interfere with the development of the Soviet science of international law.... The aim must not only be knowledge of what exists in international law but active participation in changing it."

The tendency of Soviet jurists to think in terms of a Western-dominated United Nations long after that had ceased to be a political reality is amply evidenced in the long-range Soviet attitudes to UN peace-keeping operations. The Soviet Union never, in fact, took kindly to the idea of UN peace keeping, which became one of the principal outlets for UN-based political activism with the Suez crisis of 1956. The legal argument advanced by the Soviet Union was that, under Article 43 of the UN Charter, sole competence to authorize and establish UN armed forces is allocated to the Security Council where, of course, the big power veto operates. The first major occasion for advancing this legal argument was the UN Middle East operation resulting from the combined British, French, and Israeli attack on Egypt and the Suez Canal area in 1956. There, the Soviet Union's position had been that the acts upon which the UN armed forces had been set up lacked legal force, since adopted by General Assembly resolution. It was in relation to the UN Congo operation, however, that the Soviet objections were the most vociferous, since the UN operation clearly redounded to the Soviet Union's political disadvantage in the end. Since the Soviet Union had itself participated in the UN Security Council debate authorizing the UN Congo armed force and had in fact voted in support of the relevant Security Council resolution of 14 July 1960 — which was approved by 8 votes, with 3 abstentions (China, France, and the United Kingdom) — it could not contest the legality of establishing the UN force. Instead, it had to concentrate its fire on the procedures actually used to form the force and on the practical activities of the force in the Congo. This the Soviet Union did, once it became clear that the UN force — under Secretary-General Dag Hammarskjöld's initiative — while it might be intended to prevent the re-establishment, with Belgian military support, of Belgian political and economic influence in the Congo in the person of the Katanga separatist leader Moïse Tschombé, would certainly not be used to establish Soviet political influence in the person of breakaway, left-leaning Premier Patrice Lumumba. The Soviet Union had reversed its earlier hard-and-fast opposition to international armed forces of whatever nature and had voted in the Security Council in favour of the UN Congo force, mainly because the anarchy that succeeded the proclamation of independence for the Congo on 30 June 1960 had set the stage for a Belgian return and had provoked the anguished joint appeal for help to the UN by Premier Lumumba and President Kasavubu. Here was one case, then, where the emotional "anti-colonialist" cluster of international legal values successfully outweighed, in Soviet thinking, the more cautious "institutional" cluster of international legal values with their clear preference for confining jurisdictional competence to authorize UN activity to the Security Council, where the big power veto could operate as a defence of vital Soviet interests.

Once disillusioned over the non-fulfilment of its original high hopes for UN action in the Congo, the Soviet Union could not afford to forget or forgive. The Soviet Union never pardoned Dag Hammarskjöld for favouring President Kasavubu and his supporters as the politically most reliable group for building a viable central government in the Congo. And so it undertook its personal vendetta against the UN Secretary-General, aimed at preventing any further extension of his term of office and ultimately at securing his replacement by a troika system of administration. The system would have seen the UN governed by a three-person board representing the West, the Soviet bloc, and the neutralist third world, and that would surely have ended the UN role as an independent political decision-making body, and stalemated it altogether.

The Soviet Union likewise refused to pay its UN General Assembly-assessed share of the UN peace-keeping operations in the Congo and the Middle East, contending in particular that the whole Congo operation, as actually conducted, was illegal. This led directly, following the World Court Advisory Opinion on Certain Expenses of the United Nations, to the United States-sponsored showdown, in the UN General Assembly at its nineteenth session in the fall of 1964, over the Soviet and French non-payment of the special financial assessments resulting from the UN Congo and Middle East operations. The United States' attempt to apply Article 19 of the UN Charter and take away the Soviet and French votes in the General Assembly so long as the special dues remained unpaid, brought the work of the General Assembly to a complete standstill until the United States finally backed down against a threatened break-up of the UN and allowed the work of the succeeding twentieth session to proceed without resolving the expenses issue. The Soviet Union and France resisted various face-saving devices designed to allow them to back down gracefully, and to this day have failed to pay the special assessments.

Beyond this, the Soviet Union maintained unyielding opposition to any suggestion of a standby UN military force. It viewed an international police force in any form as designed merely to utilize the United Nations for "colonialist" ends. In the same issue of a Soviet scientific-legal publication that characterized the present writer as one of "colonialism's theoreticians," then Canadian Prime Minister Lester B. Pearson was castigated for his support of an international police force. In the Soviet journal's words:

> Canada's Prime Minister Pearson proposes a standby peace force, "formally outside the United Nations but ready to be used at its request," "for preserving the peace; for carrying out and supervising U.N. recommendations when called on; for pacifying disturbed areas; and for putting the international police force behind international decisions." In other words, a new form of police operations by the imperialists is suggested, while "pacifying disturbed areas" apparently means suppression of the national-liberation movement.

This form of intransigent Soviet opposition, born of a doctrinal Soviet legal position and buttressed by bitter Soviet practical experience in the Congo, rendered progress in establishing standing UN emergency forces extremely difficult. It also threatened the whole principle of General Assembly-based peace keeping, even after the General Assembly had lost its "Western" flavour and become a predominantly third world arena.

Security Council measures, where they are not killed by the big power veto, are of course clearly international law, whatever their practical chances of success may be. What is the *legal* effect of UN General Assembly resolutions, now that the "new" countries are disposed to use their voting strength to attempt direct political action? Many Western lawyers, having second thoughts about the political wisdom of the General Assembly's "Uniting for Peace" resolution of 1950, are now inclined to deny the force of law to General Assembly resolutions. For *Soviet bloc* as distinct from *Soviet* jurists, General Assembly resolutions reflect the "developing juridical conscience of people," which they see as acting on governments and thus creating international law norms. Dr. Vratislav Pechota, a Czech jurist, used to cite such examples as the "principle of general disarmament" and the "principle of the final liquidation of colonialism"; he saw both as developing through successive General Assembly resolutions. Dr. Pechota differentiated "simple recommendations" and "solemn declarations" of the General Assembly, contending that the latter act upon the practice of states and thereby either engender new norms or change old norms of customary international law.

The Polish jurist, Professor Manfred Lachs (as he then was), echoed these thoughts. He spoke of General Assembly resolutions on the self-determination of states, international trade exchanges, and general disarmament, as leading to the formulation of "concrete and imperative principles" of international law. Answering some Western critics, Professor Lachs used to ask pointedly for the juridical basis of the principle of the non-orbiting of nuclear weapons in space vehicles. The Soviet Union and the United States clearly regarded the principle as mutually binding from the time of its expression in a UN General Assembly resolution of 17 October 1963. Yet where did its legal force come from, if it did not come from the General Assembly resolution? Of course, the principle was finally concretized in the Treaty on the Exploration and Use of Outer Space of January 1967 after intensive Soviet-US bilateral negotiation. But all that, I am sure Dr. Lachs would have said, was done simply *ex abundante cautela*, and was in no way necessary to the validity of a principle that had already been law for three years or more.

Perhaps the most interesting answer to this particular legal problem — an important one, because of the key it provides to more general, long-range attitudes taken by particular countries to UN organs and the UN as a whole, as arenas for the achievement of their distinctive national policies — is to be found in contemporary Soviet legal doctrine. Professor Gregory Tunkin, then Principal Legal Adviser to the Soviet Foreign Ministry, used to accord a certain deference to United Nations General Assembly resolutions but unlike his Soviet bloc, Eastern European colleagues, he tended to view such resolutions as only "subsidiary," auxiliary sources of international law. Two other Soviet juristic opinions had further nuances, however. Dr. Morozov suggested that General Assembly resolutions are a source of international law when adopted by states of the two socio-economic systems (communist and capitalist) and of all three main political groups (socialist, Western, and neutralist). Dr. Yanovsky agreed with this, but added the proviso that General Assembly resolutions agreed to by all three main political groups should also be adopted without dissenting vote.

These Soviet juristic statements were important for two reasons. First, they reaffirmed the more cautious Soviet doctrinal legal positions, which would allow the Soviet government (if the need should arise) to retreat politically and refuse to recognize "irresponsible" General Assembly resolutions as having any legal effect. Second, they proclaimed a legal principle that itself comes very close to reflecting the essential political facts of life in the contemporary world community: any international law norms that wish to lay claim to being viable must proceed from a genuine inter-systems consensus. In place of the old, positivistic, law-as-command theories, therefore, there was explicit recognition by Soviet jurists of a law-as-consensus approach, in which the emphasis must be upon bilateralism and reciprocity of interest as the basis of international law making in a pluralist world community.

4 THE UN CHARTER: TREATY OR CONSTITUTION?

Changing Rôle of the World Court

In his dissenting opinion on Certain Expenses of the United Nations — the Advisory Opinion handed down by the World Court on 20 July 1962, whose majority position precipitated the Western-sponsored action to deprive the Soviet Union and France of their vote in the UN General Assembly under Article 19 of the UN Charter — the then President of the Court, Polish jurist Judge Winiarski, formulated principles of interpretation which reveal, very dramatically, basic doctrinal differences between Soviet bloc and Western jurists as to the nature and character of the Charter. As President Winiarski commented:

> The Charter, a multilateral treaty which was the result of prolonged and laborious negotiations, carefully created organs and determined their competence and means of action.
>
> The intention of those who drafted it was clearly to abandon the possibility of useful action rather than to sacrifice the balance of carefully established fields of competence, as can be seen, for example, in the case of voting in the Security Council. It is only by such procedures, which were clearly defined, that the United Nations can seek to achieve its purposes. It may be that the United Nations is sometimes not in a position to undertake action which would be useful for the maintenance of international peace and security or for one or another of the purposes indicated in Article 1 of the Charter, but that is the way in which the Organization was conceived and brought into being. . . .

Judge Koretsky of the Soviet Union made the same point, but

even more succintly, in his own dissenting opinion in the same case:

> I am prepared to stress the necessity of the strict observation and proper interpretation of the provisions of the Charter, its rules, without limiting itself by reference to the purposes of the Organization: otherwise one would have to come to the long ago condemned formula: "The ends justify the means."

Since the majority of the World Court upheld the validity of the expenditures authorized by the General Assembly as legitimate "expenses of the Organization" within the meaning of Article 17 (2) of the Charter, it would be tempting, in political realist terms, to explain the dissenting opinions of the two Soviet bloc judges as purely *ad hoc* judicial responses to the political self-interest of their parent countries. Such a nakedly cynical interpretation, however, would ignore two very important considerations. First, the two Soviet bloc judges were not ranged as lone dissenters against the rest of the World Court in the UN Expenses Reference. It was a 9 to 5 holding, with the two Soviet bloc judges being joined in dissent by the French jurist Judge Basdevant (which, of course, might also lend itself to "political realist" interpretations of the judicial vote), but also by the two Latin American civil law jurists, Judge Moreno Quintana and Judge Bustamante y Rivero, who under no circumstances could be accused of secretly favouring the Soviet bloc and French political positions on the legality of the General Assembly's special financial assessments for the Middle East and Congo operations.

Second, and beyond this, there is a long and detailed history of Soviet and Soviet bloc doctrinal writing, since the establishment of the United Nations in 1945, which directly accords with the position of President Winiarski and Judge Koretsky in the UN Expenses Reference, and from which, indeed, their opinions may be said directly to flow. Summarized briefly, this long-term Soviet doctrinal legal position, vis-à-vis the United Nations, has been that the UN Charter is merely a treaty — a multilateral treaty at that — which for certain limited purposes may operate to restrict the national sovereignty of its individual national signatories. Like all treaties or other international arrangements purporting to restrict national sovereignty, however, it is to be construed strictly and, in any case, against those arguing for the restriction of national sovereignty. Such an intellectual position corresponds to those intellectual legal attitudes found in English-speaking common law countries, which insist that statutes, particularly those derogating from the civil liberties of the private citizen, are to be construed strictly and, in any case, against the claimed derogation from the private citizen's rights. It is reflected, again, in President Winiarski's further comments in the UN Expenses Reference. In reply to the legal argument that the course of actual practice at the General Assembly warranted the World Court's accepting that a new legal gloss had effectively been created upon the Charter in supplement to the bare bones of its actual text, he stated:

> Reliance has been placed upon practice as providing justification for an affirmative answer to the question submitted to the Court. The technical budgetary practice of the Organization has no bearing upon the question, which is a question of law. . . .
>
> It is . . . difficult to assert, in the case before the Court, either that practice can furnish a canon of construction warranting an affirmative answer to the question addressed to the Court, or that it may have contributed to the establishment of a legal rule particular to the Organization, created *praeter legem*, and, still less, that it can have done so *contra legem*.

The countervailing intellectual legal approach to that of President Winiarski, Judge Koretsky, and their colleagues in dissent, is that favoured by a number of Western jurists and summed up, in terms of distinctive Western municipal law attitudes, in the celebrated dictum of the great Chief Justice John Marshall of the United States Supreme Court: "Never forget that it is a constitution that we are expounding!" The essence of this particular approach is the conception that law is not a frozen doctrine whose meaning jelled once and for all in some bygone age; instead, it is a continuing process of creative adjustment of old rules and principles to rapidly changing societal interests and expectations. The importance of the statute/constitution dichotomy lies in the fact that, with an ordinary statute — which is presumably capable of fairly easy amendment by direct legislative action — it may be reasonable to expect the interests in certainty to rank very highly. This is not the case with a constitution which, by definition, is intended to endure through the ages without too many formal changes, and which therefore needs a very wide amplitude of interpretation if it is to accommodate radically new societal problems.

Those who prefer to view the UN Charter as a constitution and not a mere statute, insist that it must constantly be reexamined in the light of its original grand design as an instrument for maintaining world peace; and that the bald text of the Charter must therefore be supplemented, and literal interpretation eschewed, in favour of policy interpretations that will refine and restate the details to accord with those ultimate historical purposes and objectives.

In retrospect, neither the Soviet nor the Western policy preferences — yielding radically different sorts of answers to the basic type of problem solving that the United Nations has been concerned with since its formation in 1945 — are really very surprising. For each choice, Soviet and Western, is an example of instrumental legal thinking. In the case of the Soviet Union, strict and literal interpretation as a methodological approach to construction of the Charter was especially attuned to the defensive tactics that the Soviet Union felt obliged to use in an era when the Soviet Union and its political associates represented a tiny minority who were consistently and repeatedly outvoted by hostile, Western-dominated coalitions in the UN policy-making organs. Because the major Western countries seemed to have comfortable, pro-Western voting majorities in all main policy-making organs right from the outset, they could confidently indulge in broad, policy-making, legislative approaches to the UN Charter, secure in the knowledge that any creative rewriting or redefinition of the Charter's provisions, or any new gloss created upon its text, would not be inimical to vital Western interests. It is in this sense that some prominent Western jurists vigorously championed the legality of the UN Security Council action taken during the Korean crisis in the summer of 1950, in the absence of the Soviet representative, and the General Assembly's "Uniting for Peace" resolution adopted shortly thereafter, as examples of creative reinterpretation of the UN Charter in the full spirit of its original historical purposes. At the same time, Soviet jurists challenged these actions as unwarranted departures from the strict provisions of the Charter and as gross violations, therefore, of international law. And we saw the same essential differences of opinion, between Western and Soviet jurists, over the UN expenses issue.

The point is, of course, that an intellectual dichotomy of this sort — between purposive, policy-oriented interpretation on the one hand, and literal interpretation on the other — is as common in our own national, constitutional law as in international law. Policy-oriented interpretations are, perhaps, more palatable in internal, municipal law where there will normally be sufficient societal consensus to approve and ratify the constitutional rewriting that in fact is being invoked, in the name of a "policy interpretation," to adjust old positive law to new societal conditions. Such a general societal consensus hardly existed in the world community of the cold war era, characterized as it was by political-military bipolarity and ideological conflict in general. In such circumstances, modesty would seem called for in any attempt to force through startling new changes in the pre-existing cold war "ground rules" in the name of a "policy interpretation" of the Charter. There may have been merit, at the time, in the Soviet juristic criticism of an inherent subjectivity in Western approaches to interpretation of the Charter. As a younger Soviet jurist, writing in the Soviet Yearbook of International Law, declared:

> The main arguments of the Western jurists are based on the theory of the so-called inherent capacity, "implied powers," and the "principle of efficacy." The advocates of this theory justify any breach of the Charter by counterposing the articles which define the purposes and principles of the Organization to articles which lay down the procedure of activity and delimit the competence of organs designated for achieving these purposes. The latter, in the opinion of bourgeois jurists, can be overlooked because they supposedly are of a purely technical, procedural nature.

Distinctive national attitudes to the UN Charter and to whether it should be viewed as a mere statute (treaty) to be restrictively interpreted or instead as a constitution, have tended, in the years since establishment of the United Nations in 1945, to be parallelled by distinctive national attitudes to the World Court, and to its jurisdiction and special competence in a world community in the process of rapid and fundamental change. In our own internal, municipal law there are two main competing conceptions of the proper role of a constitutional court. One view is that a Supreme Court has a purely limited, dependent position in the general constitutional structure. It should construe its rôle narrowly, exercise self-restraint, and thus immunize itself as much as possible from great political *causes célèbres*. The other view is that, where there are practical breakdowns on the part of the main, executive and legislative organs of community policy making, the judges should move in boldly to fill the gap and to legislate, in effect, interstitially. Here we have judicially-based activism in the cause of effective community policy making.

Both these conceptions of the judical function — judicial self-restraint and judicial activism — were advanced by international lawyers in regard to the World Court in the early, post-World War II years. Soviet jurists, responding to the political fact of Soviet bloc judges being a tiny minority in an essentially Western tribunal, tended to argue the merits of judicial self-restraint; they asserted that the World Court should avoid any overt policy-making, legislating, activist rôle. Western jurists, in spite of a certain governmental fear of submitting to the compulsory jurisdiction of the Court — this a response, normally, to internal, neo-isolationist forces in their own countries, as with the so-called Connally Amendment reservation to the United States' adherence to the Court's jurisdiction — tended to be far more confident and enthusiastic about the affirmative possibilities for the Court's law-making, legislative rôle.

By the time of the landmark decision rendered by the World Court in July 1966, on the complaint by Ethiopia and Liberia against the Union of South Africa in respect to the Southwest Africa Mandate, these intellectual attitudes had become strangely blurred and scrambled. This change was a response, in measure, to vast changes in the United Nations as a whole, and particularly in the General Assembly, as a result of the flood of "new," Afro-Asian countries. The disappearance of the pro-Western majority in the General Assembly, and the further presaging of widespread changes in the make-up and composition of the World Court itself as the new forces began to marshal their voting strength effectively in the periodic election of judges, were reflected in the crossing of former intellectual lines in the World Court in the *South West Africa* case.

The actual decision of the World Court in the *South West Africa* case was achieved by a bare majority of one. The President, Australian judge Sir Percy Spender, exercised his right to cast a second, tie-breaking vote, when the Court first deadlocked 7 to 7 (this included Sir Percy's first vote as an ordinary member of the Court). The decision of the World Court, it must be said, had ample precedent in the domestic jurisprudence of most legal systems, whether common law or civil law. Courts do have the right to avoid ruling on substantive legal issues by deciding on narrow procedural points: judicial self-restraint is a recognized legal virtue in many countries, both Western and communist, especially where great political *causes célèbres* are involved. And, on the record of their performances on the World Court and in their pre-Court careers, there is nothing that warrants a partisan interpretation that the individual judges in the World Court majority gave a purely *ad hoc*, personal, political response to the substantive policy issue involved in the *South*

West Africa case. The intellectual position of the President, Sir Percy Spender, accorded with the general legal thinking of a leader of the Equity bar, which Sir Percy at one time was. It also accorded with the special legal philosophy of judicial self-restraint and practical limits to the rôle of a Supreme Court judge, developed by the late Mr. Justice Felix Frankfurter of the United States Supreme Court, who strongly influenced Sir Percy Spender in his general legal ideas when he was Australian Ambassador to the United States in the years immediately prior to his election to the World Court in 1957.

It is especially worthy of note that the Polish member of the World Court, Judge Winiarski, chose to part company with the Soviet member, Judge Koretsky, and join Sir Percy Spender in helping to form the court majority. In Judge Winiarski's case, the basic, Soviet bloc, legal view that it was unwise for the World Court to indulge in any policy-making, legislating, "political" rôle in an era of ideological division in the world community prevailed over any immediate temptation to establish a special exception and cast a triumphantly "anti-colonialist" vote in the South West Africa case.

Nevertheless, it must be said that the manner and form in which the World Court decision was rendered in the South West Africa case must be considered something of a disaster for the general cause of world law. For the actual, narrow procedural point on which the World Court majority managed to decide the case, thereby avoiding a ruling on the substantive legal issues — including the burning issue of the compatibility of the Union of South Africa government's apartheid programme with international law — would even baffle the intellectual ingenuity of the mediaeval schoolmen.

This narrow procedural point, accepted by the World Court majority in the South West Africa case, was that while the complainants, Ethiopia and Liberia, did have legal standing to bring the suit — this had been upheld in 1962, by a fifteen-man World Court by an 8 to 7 vote, with Sir Percy Spender dissenting — the two complainant African states did not have legal standing to obtain a decision in the matter. It is not too much to say that if the fifteenth member of the World Court, Judge Badawi of the United Arab Republic, had not died suddenly in 1965 (he had still not been replaced at the time of the final decision in July 1966), the 7 to 7 tie that was broken, against the complainant African states, by Sir Percy Spender's tie-breaking vote would have been 8 to 7 in favour of the complainants.

The angry charges of certain African delegates, after the announcement of the *South West Africa* decision, that the World Court was a "white man's" court, and that the emergent countries could not expect their rights to be vindicated by *legal* action that involves recourse to a "white man's" international law, were not new. They were heard in the speeches of Afro-Asian delegates in the United Nations Special Committee on Friendly Relations (Coexistence). What was new, perhaps, was the vehemence of the comments being directed against the World Court and its members, and the clamant character of the demands for direct, political action, instead of recourse to legal machinery.

Would the World Court have been better advised to delay its decision still further, though the matter had been before it for six years? The Court itself is the sole judge of the timing and staging of its decisions. Like the *Dred Scott* decision of the United States Supreme Court, which hastened the onset of the American Civil War, the World Court might be accused of having given a legally correct, but politically unwise, even irresponsible decision which other people, as well as the Court itself, would have to live with. For one immediate consequence of the decision, anticipated by certain foreign ministries, was to jeopardize prospects for ensuring that only jurists of genuine intellectual calibre and professional integrity would be nominated to, and elected to, the Court in the future. The periodical elections to the Court have always been somewhat cynical in character, even on the part of those major Western nations that officially are most committed to the Court and to extension of its jurisdiction. But the elections to the World Court in the fall of 1966, which immediately followed the *South West Africa* decision — in spite of some genuinely outstanding choices like the near unanimous selection of the Polish jurist Manfred Lachs, in succession to his fellow countryman Judge Winiarski, who had joined with Sir Percy Spender and the majority in the *South West Africa* case — was characterized by a certain meanness of spirit and outlook, and by naked political power plays attempted and actually brought off. Thus, the Australian jurist Sir Kenneth Bailey, who had distinguished himself through many years of service in UN committees and specialist agencies and who was generally considered a "professional," "UN family" choice for the Court, was beaten in his election attempt because (it was widely conceded at the time) of a third world decision to exact a form of retroactive punishment against his fellow countryman, Sir Percy Spender, for his double majority vote in the *South West Africa* case. Feelings within third world delegations ran high immediately after the *South West Africa* decision, when the periodic elections of judges to the Court came round again in the General Assembly and Security Council. History may well record that the American member of the Court, Judge Philip Jessup, more correctly sensed the "winds of change" in Africa and the general movement of world history when, in his dissenting opinion in the *South West Africa* case, he refused to evade the substantive issue of the legality of governmentally-practised racial discrimination. In categorizing the World Court majority position as "completely unfounded in law," Judge Jessup insisted that international law should not be treated as an outdated collection of dead rules, from some bygone era of world history, but that it "must take account of the views and attitudes of the contemporary international community." On this approach, Judge Jessup concluded: "The accumulation of expressions of condemnation of *Apartheid* are proof of the pertinent contemporary international standard."

In the end, the remedy of the Afro-Asian countries for the political impasse created by the World Court's denial of jurisdiction on the substantive issue in the *South West Africa* case was, after all, direct political action in the General Assembly where their voting strength could best be utilized. By a vote of 114 to 2 (with 3 abstentions) in late October 1966, the UN General Assembly voted to declare the Union of South Africa's original, League of Nations-derived mandate to administer South West Africa "terminated," and to declare that the territory now came under "the direct responsibility" of the United Nations. These were bold words, of course, and how much they would mean in fact would depend on the practical measures taken to give effect to them. While the African states, in general, wished to establish immediately a UN Administering Authority for South West Africa, the Latin American nations moved successfully to substitute a fourteen-member, *ad hoc* committee to recommend, by April 1967, "practical means" for UN administration of the territory.

The World Court was given another chance — and as some of the Court's critics indicated in advance, a *last* chance — to examine the South West Africa mandate question when the Security Council voted in 1970 to request the Court for an Advisory Opinion on the "legal consequences for States of the continued presence of South Africa in Namibia (South West Africa)." Before it could reach the substantive issues involved, the Court had to deal with some major procedural issues, including the legality of the very Security Council Resolution that had requested the Advisory Opinion. In the actual vote in the Security Council, two of the permanent members of the Council had abstained. It was argued, in consequence, that the resolution had not been adopted by "an affirmative vote of nine members including the concurring votes of the permanent members," as required by Article 27 (3) of the UN Charter for resolutions on substantive matters. The Court disposed of this particular objection by taking note of Security Council practice: over a long period, presidential rulings and the statements of Council members, particularly permanent members, had consistently interpreted voluntary abstentions by permanent members as constituting no bar to the adoption of resolutions. A far more serious objection to the Court's jurisdiction was that the question now posed to the Court by the Security Council really related to an existing dispute between South Africa and other states. Thus, the present approach to the Court was simply an attempt to do indirectly by the Advisory Opinion route, what could not be done directly by the contentious jurisdiction route (since the consent of one of the parties to the dispute, South Africa, was lacking). In holding in favour of its own jurisdiction in an Advisory Opinion proceeding, the Court had to distinguish a major precedent established in 1923 by its predecessor under the League of Nations, the old Permanent Court of International Justice, in the *Eastern Carelia* question. There the old Court had refused to accept jurisdiction, via the Advisory Opinion route, in a territorial dispute involving Finland and the Soviet Union. The Soviet Union was not a member of the League of Nations at the time and did not appear before the Court. This was the point which the Court in the *Namibia (South West Africa)* proceeding seized upon as the basis for its rather ingenious method of distinguishing the earlier, *Eastern Carelia* precedent: South Africa was a member of the United Nations, had participated in both the written and oral proceedings, and had also, while raising specific objections against the competence of the Court, addressed itself to the merits of the question.

The Court in *Namibia (South West Africa)* also had to face a series of objections, raised by South Africa, that held implications for the traditional concepts of judicial neutrality and independence, and for their meaning or relevance today when judges are increasingly called upon to transcend the limits of legal positivism and venture "legislative," "policy" interpretations. One such objection concerned the South African Government's request as a party to a legal question actually pending who was not already represented on the Court, to be allowed to name an *ad hoc* judge under the existing Rules of Court. Further objections raised by the South African Government contested the right to sit on the Court, in the present proceedings, of three of the regular judges — Judge-President Zafrullah Khan, Judge Padilla Nervo, and Judge Morozov — because of their past, active involvement in various activities within the United Nations that had been directed against South Africa. All of these South African objections were disposed of by the Court, though not without dissenting votes (3 and 5 dissenting votes, respectively, on different aspects of the *ad hoc* judge issue; 4 such votes on one, at least, of the requests for a judicial disqualification). The majority's reasoning in its official Opinion of Court is rather unsatisfying on these points, no doubt because the Court, in an evident period of intellectual transition, felt somewhat ambivalent on the choice between its more traditional functions and the contemporary political demands that it assume a more consciously creative rôle in the making of the new international law. An opportunity seems to have been missed, here, for an intellectual rationalization of the proper balance between canons of judicial self-restraint and judicial activism.

When the substantive issues were finally reached in *Namibia (South West Africa)*, after the procedural issues had been disposed of, there was a marked contrast between the lopsided votes — 13 to 2 and 11 to 4, on the two main issues — and the plethora of individual judicial opinions, ten in all. But by and large the official Opinion of Court and the individual judicial opinions are imaginative and innovative, and venture significant advances in existing legal doctrine. The Court reached out for the concept of inter-temporal law and the time dimension in legal interpretation to conclude that, whatever the character of a League of Nations mandate given to South Africa over the former German South West Africa colony in 1919, progressive, generic interpretation dictated that such a mandate be regarded as evolutionary, rather than static, particularly in respect to that "sacred trust of civilization" that mandates connoted. In the Court's view, this left little doubt that the ultimate objective of the "sacred trust" was the self-determination and independence of the peoples concerned. In the final result, then, the Court majority does seem to embrace, at last, the cause of judicial law making. This analysis of the outcome of *Namibia (South West Africa)* seems confirmed by the dissenting opinion of Judge Fitzmaurice, who had played such a key rôle in the earlier, 8 to 7, Court decision in South West Africa, Second Phase in 1966. In an annex to his dissenting opinion in Namibia, Judge Fitzmaurice went out of his way to approve the comments of Manley Hudson — a one-time American judge on the old, League of Nations era, Permanent Court of International Justice — on the need for the Court to keep "within the limits which characterize judicial action," especially in Advisory Opinion jurisdiction, and to act "not as an 'academy of jurists' but as a responsible 'magistrature.' "

The dichotomy between more orthodox, judicial self-restraint and the newer imperatives of judicial activism in aid of the "new" international law has been reflected within the ranks of the Court since Namibia was decided in 1971. There have been alternating displays of caution and confidence on great policy issues which the changes in judicial personnel, through periodic elections to the Court, do not fully explain. Rather, the Court — taking note of its own politically dependent character and its quite limited jurisdictional possibilities in relation to the powerful national Supreme Courts (the United States Supreme Court, for example), which are often suggested to it as ideal models — seems to be aware of the complexity of the judicial decision-making act and the need for some trial-and-error experimentation, in actual cases, before defining a new rôle for itself in a United Nations that has lost its Western voting majority once and for all, and effectively become a third world forum.

In the French Nuclear Tests cases, the Court seemed to have a glorious, ready-made opportunity for placing itself on the side of the angels. In ruling on the legality of high-altitude nuclear test explosions in the South Pacific, it passed up that chance in two successive decisions — an interim decision in 1973 and a final decision in 1974 — that are marked by the highly technical, procedural character of the Court and individual judicial holdings, and (once again) by the plethora of individual judicial opinions within closely divided courts. The key judicial holding, in the final judgement in 1974, was that the issue had become moot with the unilateral declarations of intention by the French President and by French ministers, indicating the termination of any further above-the-ground nuclear tests by France in the South Pacific. This particular judicial holding is at once innovative in terms of legal doctrine and conservative in that it applies the doctrine of self-restraint and avoids ruling on substantive, policy issues where lesser, procedural issues can provide a solution. The dossier in French Nuclear Tests was not completely satisfactory for purposes of a major policy ruling by the Court. The key complainant, Australia, had itself cooperated enthusiastically in American and British nuclear test explosions in the South Pacific region for many years, until a fortuitous change of government. There was also a not altogether explained incident involving an unauthorized "leak" by the Australian Prime Minister of the Court's interim ruling of 1973, prior to its official release by the Court.

The next Court ruling was *Western Sahara*, rendered only a year later. Once again the Court's judgement was accompanied by a plethora of individual judicial opinions, and this in a case where the verdict was reached by lop-sided judicial majorities. However, in *Western Sahara* the openings of judicial activism are patent and unequivocal, perhaps because the occasion — a conflict between "old" international law categories invoked by a European "colonial" power, and "new" international law principles invoked by third world, "decolonized" countries — presented the occasion for a clear-cut policy choice where *French Nuclear Tests*, as a dispute between wholly Western, post-industrial, "colonial" societies, did not. The issue of the legal title to former Spanish colonies in the Western Sahara (Rio de Oro and Sakiet El Hamra) provided, in fact, the opportunity for a far-reaching re-examination and updating of classical international law rules on the acquisition of territorial title by colonization, in respect to lands previously occupied by non-European, indigenous or aboriginal peoples (*terra nullius*). The issue came to the Court by way of a UN General Assembly request for an Advisory Opinion. The colonial power, Spain, in anticipation of UN action, had announced a decision to hold its own referendum within the colony; this move was viewed by the neighbouring third world countries and potential successor states — Morocco, Mauritania, and Algeria — as a clever stratagem designed to maintain Spain's political and economic influence over the Western Sahara after its by now inevitable decolonization and independence. The individual judicial opinions annexed to the Court's holding in *Western Sahara* have an importance that transcends the particular issues of that case. Was the Western Sahara territory, at the time of its colonization by Spain, *terra nullius*? The Court noted that Spain itself relied, for its original claim to title, on agreements, "documents," and "deeds of adherence" signed by the chiefs of the local communities with Spain and confirmed by the King of Spain; for these reasons alone, the argument that the Western Sahara was *terra nullius*, at time of colonization, would be refuted. But three of the specially concurring judicial opinions, in particular, go beyond the necessities of the case to dispose of the concept of *terra nullius* itself — those of Vice-President Ammoun, Judge Forster, and *ad hoc* Judge Boni, all of them distinguished third world jurists. Vice-President Ammoun quoted the Chief Justice of the Supreme Court of Zaire, Bayona-Ba-Meya, in order to

> ... dismiss the materialistic concept of *terra nullius*, which led to this dismemberment of Africa following the Berlin Conference of 1885. Mr. Bayona-Ba-Meya substitutes for this a spiritual notion: the ancestral tie between the land, or "mother nature," and the man who was born therefrom, remains attached thereto, and must one day return thither to be united with his ancestors. This link is the basis of the ownership of the soil, or better, of sovereignty. This amounts to a denial of the very concept of *res nullius* in the sense of a land which is capable of being appropriated by someone who is not born therefrom. It is a condemnation of the modern concept, as defined by Pasquale Fiore, which regards as *terra nullius* territories inhabited by populations whose civilization, in the sense of the public law of Europe, is backward and whose political organization is not conceived according to Western norms. ... This is the reply which may be given to the participants in the Berlin Conference of 1885. ...

Vice-President Ammoun thus rejects the purely Western, ethnocentric conception of the legal modes of establishing sovereignty over territory. He cites another distinguished third world jurist, Ambassador Mohammed Bedjaoui, in the historical demonstration that the Western-based, "classical" international law rule that effective territorial title could be established by a Western colonizer through occupation of a territory inhabited by non-Western, indigenous peoples, rested on three successive legal fictions: the first developed in the Roman era, when any territory not Roman was considered *terra nullius*; the second in the epoch of the great European discoveries of "new" lands in the sixteenth and seventeenth centuries, when any territory not belonging to a Christian sovereign was considered *nullius*; and the third in the nineteenth century, when any territory not belonging to a "civilized" state was treated as *nullius* and therefore capable of appropriation by a Western colonizing state. Thus was the concept of *terra nullius* employed until the beginning of the twentieth century to justify conquest and colonization. As Judge Ammoun noted, even in the sixteenth century the great European jurist Francisco de Vittoria had protested against the application of the concept to American Indians to deprive them of their lands.

Six years earlier, in 1969, in his specially concurring opinion in *North Sea Continental Shelf*, a strictly intra-continental Western European dispute, Judge Ammoun had taken the opportunity to reject in passing the unconscious juridical "racialism" inherent in such well-accepted, "classical" international law categories as that cited in Article 38 (1) (c) of the World Court Statute — "the general principles of law recognized by civilized nations." Not merely do such categories reflect a bygone, ethno-culturally exclusive era in the world community; they are capable of having normative legal consequences in contemporary problem-situations if care is not exercised — as indicated by the dead-hand control they could still exercise in the construction, today, of legal categories like the acquisition of territorial sovereignty.

Judge Forster, in his specially concurring opinion in *Western Sahara*, echoed Judge Ammoun in his strictures upon the spatially and temporally limited, "Western" or "classical" concept of *terra nullius*. He pointed out that "It is Africa of former times which is in question, as to which it cannot arbitrarily be required that its institutions should be a carbon copy of European institutions." *Ad hoc* Judge Boni went a step further in suggesting that, in determining the character of territorial sovereignty today, the modern principle of self-determination of peoples required obligatory consultation of the inhabitants of the territory concerned.

The development of a more confidently activist judicial approach, since *Namibia (South West Africa)* in 1971 and through *Western Sahara* in 1975, indicates the enormous potentialities of judicial law making on behalf of a "new," more consciously pluralistic international law. Such judicial legislation is, however, dependent on two key elements. First, the World Court is limited in its jurisdiction and the cases it thus receives, by the requirement that states should "consent" to its jurisdiction before they are bound to submit to it. This major gap in effective jurisdiction is rendered more palatable by the fact that states may opt in advance, in a general way, to accept the compulsory jurisdiction of the Court in cases affecting them. However, some states do not accept the Court's jurisdiction at all and some (such as the United States) qualify any such general acceptance by an express reservation as to "domestic jurisdiction," which they generally insist it is their right to define. The major hope for a significant increase in the Court's work load, and thus in the Court's law-making opportunities, lies in the Advisory Opinion jurisdiction. This depends, in turn, on the political organs of the United Nations, which must have sufficient confidence in the forward-looking character of the Court to warrant the additional time involved in bringing the Court into the international problem-solving process. This brings us to the second key element — the judges. Confidence in their intellectual open-mindedness and their personal commitments to substantial change and modernization in classical international law doctrine will alone persuade organs like the UN General Assembly to look to the Court. This means a far more sustained and conscious attention to candidates' intellectual capacities and personal philosophies of law when the triennial elections to the World Court come around in the General Assembly and Security Council.

The very complexity of judicial decision making — even, or perhaps especially, with a tribunal whose members accept the commitment to conscious judicial law making — is evidenced in the Court's interim and final judgements (in December 1979 and May 1980 respectively) in the matter of *United States Diplomatic and Consular Staff in Tehran*. This case, brought by the United States against Iran, arose from the taking over of the United States Embassy in Tehran and the forcible detention of US diplomatic and consular personnel by Iranian demonstrators in November 1979, immediately after the United States Government's decision to admit the ex-Shah of Iran to the United States for medical treatment. The Iranian Government chose not to be represented before the Court.

In its interim order of December 1979, the World Court took note of a letter received from the Iranian Foreign Minister contending that the issue of the American hostages represented only

> ... a marginal and secondary aspect of an overall problem, one such that it cannot be studied separately, and which involves, *inter alia*, more than twenty-five years of continual interference by the United States in the internal affairs of Iran.

The US Government's application to the Court, in the Iranian Foreign Minister's view, could not be

> ... divorced from its proper context, namely the whole political dossier of the relations between Iran and the United States over the last twenty-five years ... in particular the *coup d'état* of 1953 stirred up and carried out by the CIA, the overthrow of the lawful national government of Dr. Mossadegh, the restoration of the Shah and of his régime which was under the control of American in-

terests, and all the social, economic, cultural, and political consequences of the direct interventions in our internal affairs.

The response of the World Court to these averments was, first of all, a technical one. It insisted that it was for the Iranian Government to bring forward all the requisite proof and clearly establish the facts alleged, to the satisfaction of the Court. This, of course, Iran had not done, since it had chosen not to present its case before the Court. The Court's second line of argument was that, even if the allegations of persistent US Government misconduct had been established, they could not be regarded as justification for Iran's conduct and a defence to the United States' claims in the present case. This conclusion was reached on the basis that the Vienna Convention on Diplomatic Relations of 1961 and the Vienna Convention on Consular Relations of 1963 provided their own built-in remedies against abuses of diplomatic privileges and immunities, by way of espionage or interference in the internal affairs of the receiving state — namely, declaring the offending diplomatic staff *persona non grata* and thus compelling their recall.

This last cited remedy was well known and well used, from the cold war era onwards, by the Soviet Union and the United States. It has certainly been practised often enough by the two bloc leaders, with almost jovial good humour, and usually on a *quid pro quo* basis. It may have been somewhat unrealistic for the Court to suggest it as a meaningful remedy in bilateral relationships other than big power ones, or in situations where the same relative parity of political-military strength does not exist. Perhaps, again, the two Vienna Conventions are already somewhat dated and unresponsive to the political facts of life of the post-cold war era, when the diplomatic missions of the big powers are actively used as agencies of quiet diplomacy to influence events within smaller countries.

The judges of the World Court were unanimous in holding that the Iranian Government must immediately end the detention of US diplomatic and consular personnel, allow them to leave Iran, and restore diplomatic premises, property, and archives to the United States. Several of them went beyond the official Opinion of Court to base such an obligation in sources outside "classical," Western-based international law. Judge Lachs, in his separate opinion, expressly cited the large number of Afro-Asian states that had ratified the two Vienna Conventions; and Judge Tarazi, in his dissenting opinion, referred to Islamic Law on the inviolability of diplomatic envoys, to the teachings of Muhammad, and to the practice of Arab states from the seventh century. Judge Lachs felt, however, that the Court majority should have applied "sound judicial economy" and not gone into the issue of Iran's obligation to make reparation, apart from the return of the diplomatic personnel, premises, and property.

Judge Tarazi, in his dissent, adverted to the Court's affirmative duty of judicial fact finding. He felt that the US Government's actions in Iran in 1953, on behalf of the Shah, were sufficiently in the public domain to have been made a subject of judicial notice. Judge Tarazi also considered that the US Government was perfectly aware its authorization for the ex-Shah to enter the United States in October 1979 "might have untoward consequences"; therefore, any responsibility on the part of the Iranian Government had to be envisaged "in the context of the revolution which took place in that country and brought about, as it were, a break with a past condemned as oppressive." Judge Tarazi was finally very critical — as was Judge Morozov in his dissenting opinion — of various US Government actions before and after the Court was seized with jurisdiction in the case: the freezing of Iranian economic assets in the US and their preparing to satisfy various US private claims, and the abortive US military operation of April 1980. All of these actions were undertaken while the Court was embarking on its deliberation prior to judgement and, in Judge Tarazi's view, they "constituted an encroachment on the functions of the Court."

In sum, the Court unanimously reaffirmed the inviolability of diplomatic personnel and premises. Though it could hardly do otherwise, since the two Conventions concerned were very recent and quite explicit, the character of the Opinion of Court and the three individual opinions is such that the principle must be considered an imperative one, ranking almost as *jus cogens*. Beyond this point, however, the individual opinions — the separate opinion of Judge Lachs and the dissenting opinions of Judge Morozov and Judge Tarazi — properly introduce additional nuances not fully present in the official Opinion of Court, and important to the progressive development of international law doctrine. This is just what special judicial opinions are supposed to do, and with proper balance in their exercise they are fully compatible with the Court's maintaining its collegial quality while it ventures on judicial law making.

5 THE ROAD TO DETENTE

Security of Territorial Frontiers

In the past, and particularly between the two World Wars, disarmament was sometimes viewed as a sort of universal panacea for the assorted ills of the world community: by persuading competing states to reduce the size of their armies or the tonnage or fire-power of their battle fleets, you could keep the peace despite the justness or unjustness of the prevailing political settlement. It was one of the great illusions of the victors of World War I that the Versailles Treaty of 1919 — an essentially one-sided peace settlement that required (in its Article 231) defeated Germany to declare its sole responsibility for the War as the basis for the humiliating postwar military occupation and absurdly exaggerated financial reparations — could be artificially maintained by tying the beneficiary "succession" states to the main wartime victors in a series of interlocking military alliances, and by hemming in the defeated powers by all sorts of verbal constraints on their power to rearm in the future. Unlike the 1815 Congress of Vienna, which aimed at a just and sensible peace for victors and defeated alike, the Treaty of Versailles imposed a Carthaginian settlement under which the enemy must be destroyed or kept down at all costs. The Congress of Vienna built a century of peace in Europe, whereas the Treaty of Versailles contained within itself the seeds of its own rapid destruction. The lesson from this experience would seem to be that effective disarmament programmes should go hand-in-hand with just political settlements, or at least with timely and equitable revisions of political dispositions.

This truth was not lost upon continental European political leaders who realized, very early, that if détente were to become meaningful and normative in inter-bloc relations, it must proceed on the two fronts at once: first, and in the absence of a comprehensive European peace treaty, with a final settlement of post-World War II, political-territorial frontiers in Central and Eastern Europe; second, with some measured or staged reduction in the sheer size and strike-power of the rival military alliances facing each other across Central Europe. It was also understood, quite clearly, that it was unreasonable to expect all this to be achieved in one blow, and that détente itself was a *process* of easing international tensions rather than any static condition of international relations. The process of détente would be furthered by an essentially step-by-step approach, through the application of empirical, problem-oriented methods on a case-by-case basis.

Continental European leaders recognized that substantial progress towards disarmament must be accompanied by progress in the related political field of territorial frontiers. The problem was how to balance the undoubted interests in stability of existing frontiers, however capriciously these may have been established in the first place, against the interests in self-determination of peoples and the claims of ethno-cultural minorities that might have been arbitrarily allocated to one national control or another through the political accidents of the postwar *de facto* settlement. The self-determination of peoples had, after all, been erected into one of the imperative principles of the "new" international law after 1945, even if its effective application seemed limited, in United Nations practice and recognition, to successful wars of national liberation mounted by Afro-Asian, third world countries against "parent," European colonial powers. As formulated in international law doctrinal terms, the principle of self-determination of peoples was expressed generally and without qualification as to regions. Why then should it be limited to historical examples of "decolonization"?

On 31 December 1963, Premier Khrushchev of the Soviet Union issued a celebrated New Year's Eve message to all heads of state, calling for the renunciation of force in territorial disputes. Western responses to the Khrushchev missive were, on the whole, rather cautious and even reserved. There was a certain imprecision of language in the Khrushchev message, which Western statesmen — understandably, perhaps, in view of certain Soviet official positions and statements on these issues in the past — may have felt to be contrived and deliberate, allowing the Soviet Union to escape any general renunciation of force in future, and make exceptions like "wars of national liberation," infiltration by "volunteers," and the like. From their concrete dealings with the Soviet Union, Western statesmen and jurists frequently considered the concept of "wars of national liberation" to be largely self-defining from the Soviet viewpoint.

Yet in retrospect — and this serves as a commentary on the standards of international fact finding and the general state of intelligence services during the cold war era — it really does seem now that Premier Khrushchev might have meant just what he said when he called for the renunciation of force in *territorial* disputes. For the Soviet Union, far more perhaps than at earlier periods in its history, had a very substantial stake in the sanctity of territorial boundaries, and their preservation against other than peaceful, consensual change. Certainly, the strongest support for present-day Soviet territorial boundaries, whether in postwar Europe or in Asia, where nineteenth-century czarist territorial expansionism is today being actively and publicly disputed by Communist China, lies in traditional or classical international law doctrine, preferably not too flexibly or imaginatively applied. Old territorial treaties or agreements, originally assisted by military occupation or the presence of superior military power, are to be governed today by the principle of *pacta sunt servanda* — strict observance — without too many latter-day second thoughts in terms of radical international law innovations like the Soviet-developed special exception of "unequal treaties." "Unequal treaties" — meaning treaties where there was a gross disproportion in bargaining power between the two sides — are, by definition, not binding at law. The Soviet Union developed this special legal concept to free itself from the Treaty of Brest-Litovsk (made by Lenin with Imperial Germany in 1917 to take Russia out of World War I), and from other onerous treaty obligations that dated either from czarist days or from the immediate, post-revolutionary years when the Soviet's power was weak. For all practical purposes, however, the Soviet Union seems to regard the concept of "unequal treaties" as dead today, and in any case unavailable for legal use against itself in any contemporary problem-situation.

Likewise, the Western-favoured, international legal doctrine of *clausula rebus sic stantibus* — meaning the need for treaties to be interpreted and applied with regard to the background political, social, and economic facts against which they were signed and the changes in those same facts — is viewed by Soviet jurists with disdain or outright hostility. Simple *occupatio*, in relation to territorial claims, on this view derives strength from long-time user and control, uncluttered by contemporary heretical notions as to self-determination or the necessity for the consent of the indigenous populations. The principle of self-determination tends to be reserved by Soviet jurists as a privilege of "colonial" peoples, whom Soviet jurists limit more or less exclusively to historical, Western European colonization in Asia, Africa, and the Caribbean.

It seems possible, then, that Premier Khrushchev's New Year's Eve message of 31 December 1963 was far more serious than a mischievous attempt to embarrass and confuse the West in an area where the West (taking note of the substantial overseas, "colonial" holdings — past and present — of a number of members of NATO and the Western military alliance) had traditionally been at a profound psychological and political disadvantage. This conclusion is strengthened by recourse to Soviet scientific legal writing, both before and after Premier Khrushchev's message. These writings revealed a sustained Soviet intellectual campaign to legitimate both the current Soviet territorial frontiers and the *de facto* political-military frontiers of 1945 in Central Europe. There was also a substantial and carefully designed attempt to anticipate any Chinese Communist claim that existing Sino-Soviet territorial boundaries should be revised, based on a Soviet-style "unequal treaties" argument. For part of the Soviet drive in the scientific legal literature was to enumerate, with great public pride, historical examples of renunciation by the Soviet Union — of its own free will and at its own initiative — of treaties from the era of czarist Russia that violated the rights of peoples in Asian countries. The clear implication was that any and all such treaties had long since been denounced by the Soviet Union.

It seems clear today that Premier Khrushchev's New Year's Eve message was a Soviet defensive or anticipatory move directed against Communist China. When their advisers on Soviet affairs failed to read the signals correctly, Western political leaders misconstrued the Soviet leader's action as simply a continuation of cold war manoeuvring for political advantage. Because of this, and also because of a certain timorousness on the part of Western policy makers immediately after President Kennedy's death, a certain opportunity may have been lost for legally consolidating with the Soviet Union — on a reciprocal, formal basis — that quite considerable investment in settled expectations and historical continuity in the legal development and accomplishment of social change that customary international law, properly applied, is supposed to assist.

The Yalta Declaration of February 1945 had set the patterns for dismembering Germany and for generally settling the political map of Central and Eastern Europe. The Declaration stipulated that unconditional surrender would be imposed on Nazi Germany, with a central allied Control Commission headquartered in Berlin and separate military occupation zones administered by the United States, Great Britain, France, and the Soviet Union. It also provided for major accessions of territory from defeated Germany in the north and the west to a newly restored Poland, in compensation for Poland's giving up major portions of its prewar, eastern territories to the Soviet Union. The new Polish-Soviet frontier would move substantially westwards and follow the old, short-lived, Curzon Line of 1919, these arrangements being confirmed in the Potsdam Agreement of August 1945 following Germany's final defeat. It is a matter of record that, with the breakdown of the short-lived "victors' consensus" of 1945 and the onset of the cold war, the three Western military powers consolidated their individual zones of occupation into one (Western) territorial unit to which sovereignty was restored in 1949, accompanied by the adoption of a new federal constitution, the Bonn (or West German) constitution. The Soviet Union followed a similar course in its own zone of military occupation, and conferred sovereignty on the zonal administration and a new East German (German Democratic Republic) state. These two, parallel actions no more than consolidated the existing political-military facts of life in Central and Eastern Europe at War's end in May 1945.

There were some attempts by the Soviet Union, even after the formation of the two German states in 1949, to offer the prospect of a reunited, all-German state if West Germany would stay out of the Western military alliance and resist economic integration into Western Europe. However, these blandishments were disposed of by the early 1950s, when the Adenauer administration in West Germany opted for the abortive European Defence Community but also for the vibrant and soon visibly successful European Coal and Steel Community, the forerunner of the present-day supra-national European Community. The frontier issue in Central and Eastern Europe remained potentially disturbing, however, in the absence of an acknowledged *de jure* base in any general, pan-German peace treaty. The territorial situation established by force of arms in 1945 and continued *de facto* thereafter, might have acquired its own form of legitimation through sheer passage of time and long-time user and state practice. This is the proposition, first advanced by

Jellinek, of the normative quality of the factual. But purely *de facto* legal conditions have a habit of inviting outside intervention, and this danger was increased in the case of the two Germanies by the existence of that major "gap" in the United Nations Charter, the so-called "enemy state" provisions (Articles 53 and 107), which expressly authorized action by the World War II victors against their defeated enemies, outside and not subject to control by the UN Charter.

The potentially dangerous situation in the two Germanies held, always, the danger of escalation into a political and military confrontation between the big powers because of their common physical presence in Berlin. This was a divided city which, from the Western viewpoint, constituted a Western political enclave in the heart of the Soviet zone. Politically and legally, it had the most ambiguous status of all. At two points in time — at the end of the 1940s when the Soviet Union mounted a land blockade around West Berlin that could only be countered by a massive and costly Western airlift of supplies, and at the beginning of the 1960s when the East Berlin administration constructed the famous "Berlin Wall" to seal off contacts between the Eastern and Western sections of the city — Soviet-Western tensions seemed to threaten actual military conflict.

The ending of all the legal ambiguities and political dangers in the two-Germanies situation was made possible by the coincidence of two events. The first involved the "conservative" tendency of Soviet foreign policy to try and make assurance doubly sure by legitimating in *de jure* terms what might, for all practical purposes, be beyond legal doubt. The Soviet Government launched a vigorous campaign for a final settlement of the territorial question in Eastern and Central Europe, and made it a key and continuing element in its approach to détente. Since, by this time, concrete steps were being taken by the East and West to control nuclear weapons and weapons testing, there was a certain temptation, on each side, to link concessions on the recognition of frontiers to further and substantial concessions on disarmament.

Secondly, political events within West Germany — the "Grand Coalition" of Christian Democrats and Socialists in the mid-1960s, the development of a new consensus politics on foreign policy including the Brandt *Ostpolitik*, and a certain impatience with the continuing impasse in East-West relations — promoted an opening to the Soviet Union and Eastern Europe. Less absolutist in his basic methods than his predecessors, West German Foreign Minister and later Chancellor Willy Brandt applied a new "politic of little steps" in regard to Eastern Europe. The frontiers question was, in fact, finally regulated by a series of complementary, usually bilateral agreements concluded between, for the most part, the West German Government and individual Soviet bloc governments in Eastern Europe. Considerable legal ingenuity was required to conclude these accords — apart from political imagination and civil courage as between old enemies — since the two Germanies did not recognize each other at international law. There were also special complications, for example, in West German-Czech relations and in the retroactive legal negation of the infamous Munich Agreement of 1938, as demanded on the Czech side. Though certain elements of this "politic of little steps" required the participation of the three Western military occupation powers in addition to that of the Soviet Union to be legally effective, the original and main initiative was intra-European, West German and Soviet, within the general framework of emerging détente. Taken together, this series of East-West accords and agreements constitutes a body of interlocking legal principles defining the juridical status of the territorial frontiers once and for all. The "politic of little steps" achieved its first concrete manifestation in the West German-Soviet Non-Aggression Treaty signed in Moscow in August 1970. It was quickly followed by the West German-Polish Treaty concerning Basis for Normalizing Relations signed in Warsaw in November 1970, the Quadripartite (Britain, France, United States, Soviet Union) Agreement and Notes on Berlin signed in Berlin in September 1971, the Treaty on Basis of Relations between the Federal Republic of Germany and the German Democratic Republic signed in East Berlin in December 1972 (the so-called *Grund Vertrag* or Basic Treaty), and the West German-Czechoslovak Treaty establishing Normal Relations between the Two Countries signed in Prague in December 1973.

There is no doubt that these generally bilateral, East-West treaties and accords are legally sufficient in themselves to settle the Central and Eastern European frontiers question on a *de jure* basis. The umbrella-type accord that followed two years later, in the Final Act of Helsinki of 1 August 1975, on this view adds nothing new of a legal character on the frontiers questions. It is an act of legal supererogation. Indeed, because of the frequent looseness and vagueness of its drafting — compared to the remarkable succinctness and precision of the individual, *Ostpolitik* mini-accords of 1970 to 1973 — the Helsinki Final Act introduces a whole range of new East-West problems while purporting to bury the old ones. Part of the problem with the Helsinki Final Act arose from the sheer number of participants at the Helsinki Conference. A limited (NATO-Warsaw Pact) negotiating group of nineteen states was enlarged to thirty-five states, including some purely trivial or nominal states. The jump in numbers involved not merely a quantitative but a qualitative change, bringing unfortunate tendencies to speak to the gallery and one's own home political audience rather than concentrating on concrete problem solving, and to drag in too many favourite hobby-horses not strictly germane to the stated Conference purpose of the regulation of security and cooperation within Europe. Would it have been better, assuming that some final symbolic act was considered legally necessary to "crown" the highly successful *Ostpolitik* mini-accords, to have limited the participants to those European countries directly concerned — the actual signatories to the 1970-1973 accords? International law considerations going back to the legal consequences of Germany's unconditional surrender in 1945 dictated, no doubt, that the participants be expanded from the original Central and East European "special community" to include the other three, Western members of the Big Four — Britain, France, and the United States — in addition to the Soviet Union. Once the military factor was admitted, then the expansion to include all of NATO (non-European as well as European members) as well as all of the Warsaw Pact countries became logical, as did perhaps the admission of non-Alliance, neutral states like Finland, Ireland, Sweden, and Switzerland. Opening the doors, then, to the European mini-states and quasi-states — like Cyprus, Malta, Liechtenstein, Monaco, San Marino, and The Vatican — was simply a *reductio ad absurdum* for an all-European conference, though these countries generally proved modest in their interventions. The major conflict in the Helsinki Conference and the Helsinki Final Act, a Pandora's Box of future problems for the cause of East-West détente, sprang from the United States' decision to make human rights a major substantive issue going beyond the more limited (reuniting of families and relatives across Central and East European political frontiers) questions treated in the *Ostopolitik* mini-accords. For in seeking to examine larger issues of the Soviet Government's internal treatment of political and religious minorities and political dissidents, the West transcended the more immediate pan-European security and cooperation purpose of the Helsinki conclave, and challenged the Soviet Union in a politically sensitive area that the Soviet Union had always considered to be, in doctrinally conservative terms, wholly within its domestic jurisdiction. Secretary Brezhnev, who was generally considered the main Soviet sponsor of a pan-European security conference, and who was anxious to cap his long career with a highly symbolic act that also legitimated Soviet gains in the 1945 *de facto* political-military settlement, must have had reason to regret his own initiative.

6 TAMING THE NATIONS

Nuclear Disarmament and Arms Control

Positive suggestions for nuclear and general disarmament of the two rival blocs in Europe came with the inauguration of the de-Stalinization campaign within the Soviet Union. Characteristically, it was the imaginative young leaders in the supporting Soviet bloc countries of Eastern Europe who took the first courageous steps. Thus, Polish Foreign Minister Rapacki initiated the plan that bears his name in February 1958, with the call for a denuclearized zone in Central Europe, extending to Poland, Czechoslovakia, and the two Germanies. The Rapacki Plan prohibited the manufacture and the stockpiling of nuclear arms in that zone, and also the employment of nuclear weapons against the zone. The support of the three Western powers (the US, Britain, and France) and the Soviet Union was vital to the success of the plan, which rested on a control authority composed of representatives of NATO, the Warsaw Pact, and the non-aligned countries. After a first, negative reaction on the part of the Western powers, Foreign Minister Rapacki added, as a second phase of the plan, the reduction of classical military forces, but the plan foundered on the rock of the two-Germanies problem, as did the later and rather more modest Polish Government proposal, the Gomulka Plan, which envisaged a freezing at already existing levels of those nuclear weapons already in place in the Central European zone.

The first real breakthrough came, significantly enough, with a largely scientific agreement that was addressed only marginally to disarmament issues. The Antarctic Treaty of December 1959 was a direct product of East-West scientific and technical cooperation in the International Geophysical Year of 1958. In looking to a continuance of such scientific cooperation in the exploration and research in Antarctica, the treaty also prohibited the establishment of military bases, the testing of weapons, nuclear explosions, and the disposal of radioactive waste materials within Antarctica. The legal ban on nuclear explosions in Antarctica thus rode into history on the back of an international scientific accord, but it established useful precedents in specific areas of East-West relations, such as the use of observers to monitor treaty performance, and initiated the successful basic methodology for resolution of East-West conflicts, namely, the pragmatic, empirical, step-by-step approach.

The Antarctic Treaty was followed by the Memorandum of Understanding between the US and the Soviet Union on the establishment of a Direct Communications Link, signed in Geneva in June 1963 and generally known as the "Hot Line" Agreement. This was designed to ensure quick communication between the two bloc leaders in crisis situations, and thus avoid war through miscalculation or simple failure to communicate.

From there it was a short step to the key agreement, the Moscow Partial Test Ban Treaty of August 1963. Conceived and drafted essentially by the two bloc leaders, and then opened to signature by other states, the treaty banned nuclear weapon tests in the atmosphere, in outer space, and under water. It was followed by the Treaty on the Exploration and Use of Outer Space, including the Moon and other Celestial Bodies of January 1967. In one of its key provisions, the Outer Space Treaty rendered into formal, treaty law the principle — originally proposed jointly by the Soviet Union and the United States and already embodied in a UN General Assembly resolution of 17 October 1963 — of an undertaking not to place nuclear or other mass destruction weapons in orbit around the earth or to install them on celestial bodies. In its main substantive provisions, the Outer Space Treaty borrowed from the principles of the Antarctic Treaty in declaring outer space, the moon, and other celestial bodies to be free for investigation and exploration by all states and, as such, incapable of national appropriation. The Outer Space Treaty was later supplemented by specific conventions in the same general area: an Agreement on the Rescue of Astronauts and the Return of Objects launched into Outer Space of 1968; and a Convention of International Liability for Damage caused by Space Objects of 1972.

The step-by-step approach in the specific area of disarmament produced, as the follow-up to the Moscow Partial Test Ban Treaty of 1963, the Treaty on the Non-Proliferation of Nuclear Weapons of 1968. There were gaps in the 1963 treaty: in spite of its near universal acceptance, key countries like the

People's Republic of China still engaged in their own nuclear experiments; and France, still pursuing President de Gaulle's grand design of an independent, nuclear *force de frappe* that would not be tied to American foreign policy, did not sign the treaty. There was a still greater potential gap in the ability of the superpowers to transfer nuclear weapons to their own military allies or to neutral states over whom they might not always be able to exercise effective control. The Soviet Union viewed with expressed concern the US-sponsored Multilateral Force (MLF) under which a nuclear force, integrated into NATO and open to all its members, would be created and equipped with Polaris missiles furnished directly by the United States; the Soviet Union saw the MLF as opening the possibility that nuclear weapons might fall into West German hands. On the other hand, neutral states outside the two rival blocs became anxious about the potential expansion of membership in the nuclear "club" to countries already on the threshold of nuclear power. As early as 1958, the Republic of Ireland had introduced a resolution in the UN General Assembly calling on the existing UN Disarmament Committee to consider an international agreement, subject to inspection and control, whereby the powers producing nuclear weapons would refrain from handing over the control of such weapons to any states not possessing them, and whereby the latter states would refrain from manufacturing such weapons. This resolution was adopted a year later. Within the Eighteen-Nation Disarmament Committee, the Soviet Union and the United States — both by now concerned with maintaining the virtual monopoly on nuclear weapons enjoyed by themselves and their associates, and with preventing nuclear weapons from falling into the hands of "irresponsible" states outside the original big power nuclear club — worked closely together and eventually filed a joint text which was adopted by the UN General Assembly in mid-1968 as the Non-Proliferation Treaty by 95 votes to 4, but with 21 abstentions. In spite of this impressive vote in the General Assembly, however, gaps still remained. Some nuclear "threshold" states felt that the treaty represented effective legal discrimination between nuclear and non-nuclear states and consecrated, in international law terms, the nuclear hegemony of the two superpowers; other states complained that the treaty only prevented *horizontal* proliferation from the superpowers to lesser states, but did not control *vertical* proliferation and the amassing of more and more nuclear weapons, of ever-increasing sophistication, by the superpowers themselves. In the event, two confirmed nuclear powers — France and the People's Republic of China — and a number of key "threshold" states, neither signed nor ratified the treaty.

The step-by-step approach to disarmament — based on the reciprocal self-interest of the two bloc leaders, who jointly worked out draft treaties that were then presented to the other, lesser or supporting powers — was confirmed and extended in the Treaty on the Prohibition of the Emplacement of Nuclear Weapons and other Weapons of Mass Destruction on the Sea-Bed and the Ocean Floor and in the Subsoil thereof of February 1971; in the Convention on the Prohibition of the Development, Production and Stockpiling of Bacteriological (Biological) and Toxin Weapons of April 1972; and in the Convention on the Prohibition of Military or any other Hostile Use of Environmental Modification Techniques of 18 May 1977. These three conventions are models of the step-by-step, essentially bilateral (Soviet-US) approach to a more generally binding accord, for though they use the machinery of the Eighteen-Nation (later expanded to Twenty-Six-Nation) Disarmament Committee of the UN and eventually go back to the UN General Assembly itself for formal approval, the operational methodology and the key to ultimate success is the intensive, point-by-point, private negotiation between the Soviet Union and the United States on both general issues and their actual, detailed implementation.

The Moscow Accords of May 1972, signed by President Nixon and Secretary Brezhnev, were hailed as introducing the era of détente in East-West relations. In fact the Moscow Accords were subsequent steps in a process of détente long since begun, and substantially evidenced in a series of concrete measures — formal agreements, mutual understandings, and reciprocal patterns of conduct — over the years, between the two bloc leaders. Apart from the specific accords worked out in the step-by-step process, beginning with the Antarctic Treaty of 1959 and the Moscow Test Ban Treaty of August 1963, there were other aspects of disarmament and control of nuclear weapons that lent themselves very effectively to the same essentially modest, non-rhetorical, gradualist techniques, with results that were amply vindicated by their problem-solving record. Premier Khrushchev himself, in an interview given to United Press International in Moscow in December 1963, designated certain Soviet and Western moves of this nature, in disarmament and related areas, as the "politic of mutual example" — denoting a species of law making in Soviet-Western relations usually involving a unilateral initiative by one bloc in the confident expectation that the other bloc, by pressure of world public opinion or the like, would inevitably follow. Examples of this "politic of mutual example" can be seen in rapidly successive Soviet and Western decisions to reduce arms expenditure, to reduce uranium production, and even to close nuclear reactor plants.

On the question of military budgets and the size of armed forces, Premier Khrushchev himself suggested that certain measures could "at present be undertaken unilaterally, as a first push, so to speak." In this regard, Premier Khrushchev announced, in his December 1963 statement to United Press International's Moscow representative, that the Soviet Union had already adopted a decision to reduce military expenditures in the 1964 budget. He called on other states to do likewise, as a means of relaxing the arms race and international tension generally, through the "politic of mutual example." It is a fact, of course, that the announcement of the Soviet reductions in arms expenditure was followed almost immediately, in President Johnson's Address to Congress of 8 January 1964, by a similar American announcement of major proportions.

Of equal if not greater importance was President Johnson's initiative in the cutbacks in uranium production and the closing of atomic reactor plants. The US President had accompanied his announcement of dramatic cuts in the US military budget by a specific announcement of the curtailment in the coming year, 1964, of enriched uranium production by 25 percent, and of the shutting down of four plutonium piles. President Johnson, at the same time, called on the Soviet Union to follow the American example.

When the Soviet response seemed somewhat slow in coming, the United States renewed the proposal, and made further suggestions — not only that the Soviet Union follow the "principle of mutual example" and make similar reductions in its production of fissionable materials, but also that it agree to the "plant-by-plant shutdown of additional nuclear production facilities on a verified and reciprocal basis." When Premier Khrushchev at last replied to this American invitation in April 1964, it was to announce not merely a reduction in Soviet uranium production, but the immediate suspension of the construction of two large new atomic reactors for the production of plutonium.

Thus, for some years after the achievement of the Khrushchev-Kennedy détente in October 1962 with the peaceful resolution of the Cuban missile crisis, these policies — the step-by-step approach to resolution of Soviet-Western conflicts, and the progression by unilateral action, relying on its exemplary effect — were vindicated in a number of vital ways. (The informal, unstructured approach, proceeding essentially from executive-administrative wit and imagination, had its place in the armoury of diplomatic-legal technique alongside the more formal approach, through specific treaties. At a certain point in the whole process of détente, however, the mass of particular problem-solutions lent themselves to the establishment, by induction, of overarching general principles that would synthesize what had already been achieved, but also give more coherent direction to, and speed up, the whole process for the future. This particular moment seemed to have been reached with the planning and organization of the Nixon-Brezhnev Summit Meeting, and the actual negotiation and drafting of the Moscow Accords.)

The Moscow Accords were in reality a series of agreements, the two key ones being the Treaty on the Limitation of Anti-Ballistic Missile Systems (the so-called ABM Treaty), and the Interim Agreement on Limitation of Strategic Offensive Arms (the so-called Interim Agreement). There was, in addition, an umbrella agreement that postulated a sort of code of Soviet-US "good neighbourliness," and a series of individual agreements on such joint cooperation — in environmental protection, in the exploration and use of outer space for peaceful purposes, in medical science and public health, in science and technology, and even in the prevention of military "incidents" on and over the high seas. On these essentially secondary aspects of the Moscow Accords we need say little more, for both their purposes and their mutual benefit are evident. It is worth noting in passing, however, that the umbrella agreement on principles of Soviet-US good neighbourliness opens with an express recognition that "there is no alternative to conducting their mutual relations *on the basis of peaceful coexistence."* This statement gave the final quietus to a largely semantic quarrel that had exercised the rival foreign ministries for more than a decade, since the Soviet Union first raised the idea of big power détente under the rubric of "peaceful coexistence" and the West, in reaction, had insisted that the détente process be characterized as the pursuit of "friendly relations and cooperation among states in accordance with the United Nations Charter."

The ABM Treaty and the Interim Agreement of May 1972, taken together with two earlier (1971) and somewhat less important accords, the Agreement on Measures to reduce the risk of Outbreak of Nuclear War, and the Agreement on Measures to improve the USA-USSR Direct Communications Link, constitute what are known as the SALT I Agreements. These agreements flowed from the American intelligence services' discovery, as early as 1966, of the Soviet deployment around Moscow of an anti-ballistic missile system capable of providing limited defence against American intercontinental ballistic missiles. This would have had the effect of undermining or threatening the existing nuclear strategic balance between the Soviet Union and the United States, and would thus have compelled reciprocal development by the United States of its own anti-ballistic missile system, starting off a new and very costly Soviet-US arms race. To avoid such an unnecessary and expensive competition, a new Soviet-US agreement, leading to the ABM Treaty, was developed. The general principle of the ABM Treaty, signed in May 1972, was the limitation of ABM systems, with each side undertaking not to deploy such systems for the defence of its territory and not to provide a base for such a defence except as specifically provided in the treaty. This exception to the general prohibition of ABM systems, and in fact the treaty's key article, allowed each party to have *one* ABM system deployment area with a radius of 150 kilometres centred on its own national capital, with a limitation on the numbers of missile launchers, interceptor missiles, and radar complexes at launch sites. There was also to be one further ABM system deployment area, with similar limitations on numbers of launchers, interceptor missiles, and radar complexes, separated by no less than 1300 kilometres from the first system. In essence, the plan of the treaty was to limit the Soviet Union and the United States, henceforward, to a maximum of two ABM systems in widely separated areas of their countries.

The Interim Agreement accompanying the ABM Treaty as a key component of SALT I was, as its name implied, made for a term of years only. It was to remain in force "for a period of five years unless replaced earlier by an agreement on more complete measures limiting strategic offensive arms." In principle it aimed at banning any new construction of ICBM launchers, with numerical limits on ballistic missile submarines and submarine-launched ballistic missiles for the specified time period, pending successful completion of a permanent agreement on strategic offensive arms to accompany the ABM Treaty already signed — through what later became known as the SALT II discussions. A Protocol to the Interim Agreement added specific details on the quantitative limits, for both parties, of submarine-launched ballistic missiles and modern ballistic missile submarines. The most striking feature of these limits was that the United States accepted, thereunder, a numerical disparity in favour of the Soviet Union. This numerical disparity in missile strength was accentuated by the fact that the freezing of the levels of fixed land-based ICBM launchers established in the substantive part of the Agreement conferred a distinct advantage on the Soviet Union, which had, at the relevant date, a much greater number of such launchers — one American estimate being 1618 to 1000, and this quite apart from the Soviet Union's massive advantage in missile throw-weight. Balanced against that, the United States had, at the relevant date, a qualitative advantage in its great technical sophistication in multiple warhead technology, though it could be expected that this advantage would be overcome, in time, as Soviet missile technology caught up in the field.

A further Nixon-Brezhnev Summit Meeting in Washington in June 1973 prepared the way for the Vladivostok Summit Meeting of November 1974, carried on by President Nixon's successor, President Ford, with Secretary Brezhnev — the so-called SALT II negotiations. The continuing evolution in big power thinking on nuclear weapon strategy can be observed in the negotiating process, in the switch from Defence Secretary McNamara's "mutual assured destruction," with its emphasis on civilian targets, to a new emphasis on military targets and a new logistical realism that could accept, for example, something less than weapon parity on Secretary of State Kissinger's argument that the claimed advantages of any Soviet quantitative or missile throw-weight superiority must be discounted by the fact that the Soviet Union's weapons might be more powerful than needed for their targets.

The Vladivostock negotiations provided a general framework for a subsequent detailed agreement, still to be worked out, on strategic arms limitation. At a news conference immediately after the Vladivostok Summit Meeting, President Ford fleshed out this framework of agreement. It had been accepted that there would be a ceiling of 2400 for each side on the total number of intercontinental ballistic missiles, submarine-launched missiles, and heavy bombers; of each side's total, 1320 might be armed with multiple warheads. Immediately after the Ford news conference, the internal political debate in the United States began, with the "hard-liners" attacking President Ford's more flexible approach to a US negotiating position that would be within the range of Soviet acceptance. The November 1976, US presidential campaign stalemated all attempts to proceed to a permanent treaty during that time and, after the election of President Carter, changes in basic American foreign policy led to a deterioration in the general climate of Soviet-US détente, and a continued impasse over concretization of the SALT II negotiations in final treaty form. New disagreements emerged, at the same time, as to whether limitations should be placed on the newly-developed Soviet supersonic bomber, code-named "Backfire" by NATO officials; and on whether limitations should apply to the new American "cruise" missiles, a species of low-flying, air-breathing, unmanned missiles launchable from aircraft and submarines, and reportedly capable of landing within thirty yards of their target. Some US administration officials, notably Secretary of State Vance, began speaking of a treaty limiting nuclear armaments until 1985, and of a declaration of principles that would govern the negotiation of a future SALT III accord after the SALT II accord had been finalized. Internal disputes within the Carter administration between "hard-liners" and "soft-liners" in foreign and defence policy, and the resignation early in 1980 of Secretary of State Vance — who had been most closely associated in the public mind with the détente process and the pragmatic approach to East-West negotiations — apparently led to the United States' decision to shelve the SALT II treaties and any further, long-range talks directed to a SALT III treaty, at least until after the November 1980, presidential elections.

The apparent collapse of SALT talks did not necessarily herald any dramatic changes in either Soviet or American attitudes towards strategic arms programmes. The Interim Agreement of 1972 signed as part of the Nixon-Brezhnev Moscow Accords had expired in 1977, but both the Soviet and the US Governments had apparently continued to abide by its limits on missile launchers, with the expectation that self-restraint on one side would induce a similar reaction on the other — a further demonstration of the operational utility, in the disarmament process, of the "politic of mutual example." Just before the formal expiry of the five-year time period specified in the Interim Agreement of 1972, both Soviet Foreign Minister Gromyko and US Secretary of State Vance had, in fact, issued individual statements indicating that they would avoid taking any steps incompatible with the strategic arms limitation agreement, set to expire on 3 October 1977, if the other side would do the same. This unusual diplomatic tactic seemed to be aimed at avoiding the internal political problems that might be posed in the United States by any formal, bilateral extension of the Interim Agreement.

While the negotiations for strategic arms limitation were taking place, the search was proceeding for a mutually agreed upon, conventional military balance (at a significantly lower level of deployment and cost) between the two rival forces, NATO and the Warsaw Pact, that faced each other across Central Europe. Discussions to this end were first proposed by the Western side in 1968. In its actual origins, the quest for Mutual Balanced Force Reductions (MBFR) seems to have occurred independently of either East-West nuclear disarmament and strategic weapons negotiations, or diplomatic initiatives towards stabilization of territorial frontiers in Central and Eastern Europe. However, success in achieving NATO-Warsaw Pact reductions in military forces was so obviously complementary to the staged progress towards those other objectives, that issue "linkage" between them at various times became logical and inevitable. Once, indeed, the "politic of little steps" pursuit of security of frontiers in Europe had been achieved with the 1970-1973 *Ostpolitik* mini-accords and the Helsinki Final Act of 1 August 1975, mutual balanced force reductions between the East and West in Central Europe seemed a necessary, detailed follow-up to the principles of "All-European" security and to the military "confidence-building" measures stipulated in the Final Act.

The autonomy that the MBFR negotiations largely maintained from the beginning, related in considerable measure to the nature and character of the participants. East-West nuclear disarmament and strategic arms control started, on a serious basis, much earlier than the other main subjects of détente; and, because participation in discussions was effectively premised on membership in the "nuclear club," it was largely achieved by Soviet-US, bilateral negotiation. Similarly, the very success and rapidity (once the *Ostpolitik* programme had been finally inaugurated) of East-West frontier settlement, seemed linked to the fact that the negotiations were effectively limited to the Central and Eastern European "special community" directly concerned. In comparison the Helsinki Conference, which was opened up to "strangers" only marginally related to the questions involved, began to lose itself in a mass of extraneous issues. Any hope of an orchestrated *pas de deux* between the Helsinki Final Act and MBFR in Europe was thereby lost. Because of its unique diplomatic format as a negotiation between the members of two opposing military alliances — a throwback, in some respects, to the earlier Soviet diplomatic feelers in favour of that ultimate contradiction in terms, a "non-aggression pact" between NATO and the Warsaw Pact — the MBFR project developed its own independent momentum from the outset.

Formal negotiations did not really begin until 1973. They involved, throughout, the twelve NATO countries and the seven Warsaw Pact countries, though it was sensibly accepted that only seven NATO countries (the US, West Germany, Great Britain, Canada, and the three Benelux countries) and four Warsaw Pact countries (the Soviet Union, East Germany, Poland, and Czechoslovakia) — the only countries with military forces actually located in Central Europe — should be considered "direct participants" entitled to sign any agreement emerging from the negotiations. The basic Western negotiating position was to insist that MBFR lead, by stages, to a stable balance in Central Europe, based on parity in ground forces manpower. It should start with Soviet and American force reductions in an initial phase, and then broaden its scope to include tactical nuclear weapons. This Western approach was predicated upon recognition of existing asymmetries between NATO and Warsaw Pact forces, with the implication that greater reductions in conventional forces (notably tanks) by the Warsaw Pact could perhaps be compensated for by greater reductions of NATO tactical nuclear weapons. It was soon evident, however, that the two sides had differing perceptions of the existing relationship of forces between them. The Warsaw Pact negotiators proposed equal percentage reductions of the troops of all states concerned, rejecting NATO arguments that geographical and other asymmetries required proportionately larger Warsaw Pact reductions. The specific Warsaw Pact proposals called for reductions, in three stages and on an equal basis by the two sides, of ground, air, and nuclear forces, with ceilings on numbers of troops of the individual nations in the central region (a provision clearly aimed at limiting the size of West German forces). But the West objected to all this on the ground that it would have the effect of freezing NATO-Warsaw Pact forces in the central region on a basis that allowed clear superiority of the Soviet bloc — approximately 950,000 on the Soviet side to 800,000 on the Western side.

According to all the experiences, by the mid-1970s, of a decade and a half of East-West negotiation on the basis of reciprocity of interests, the gap separating the two sides was not so formidable. It should have been possible to bridge it, before the end of the 1970s, in a concrete agreement using the same step-by-step methods that had yielded such patent success in other, cognate areas. The fact that an MBFR treaty was not achieved by the late 1970s must be attributed to the more general deterioration in Soviet-US relations after the Helsinki Conference and the follow-up Belgrade Review Conference, and to the decline in the spirit of détente as a whole. Conclusion of an MBFR Treaty has thus been another, incidental casualty of the suspension of the SALT II Treaty ratification. However, the MBFR negotiations have not been abandoned; the talks continue, albeit on a somewhat desultory basis, and no catastrophic changes have been attempted on either side in the existing military balance in Central Europe, although some difficult new issues involving Euro-strategic armaments have emerged. The MBFR process can thus be revitalized without too much difficulty, and with the same predictable possibilities of success, as soon as the détente process as a whole recovers the momentum of the 1960s and the early 1970s.

Of related interest to the MBFR process was the long, drawn-out process finally brought to a conclusion in 1974 — the attempt to legally outlaw "aggression." Sir Austen Chamberlain, a worldly-wise and politely cynical British Foreign Secretary of the decade immediately following World War I, described the attempts to legally define and then legally proscribe aggression as a "trap for the innocent and a sign-post for the guilty." The period between the two World Wars, perhaps in reaction to the disillusionment following that most absurdly unnecessary of all wars, the First World War, involved the assiduous diplomatic pursuit of formulae for the verbal solution of great political conflicts whose substantive causes politicians were all too often either unable or unwilling to comprehend. We have seen how the Kellogg-Briand Pact, in 1928, solemnly outlawed war without attempting in any way to come to grips with the most immediate and substantial causal factor in any future war in Europe, the fundamentally unfair "victors" Peace Treaty of Versailles. And so it was with the pursuit of a legal definition of "aggression," which was brought up by Soviet Foreign Minister Maxim Litvinoff at the World Disarmament Conference in Geneva in 1933, and later studied in detail by a seventeen-nation committee headed by distinguished Greek jurist Nicolas Politis. The matter was revived by the Soviet Union at the fifth session of the UN General Assembly in 1950, referred to the International Law Commission (which returned the brief in the belief that the concept of aggression was "too complex to be susceptible to legal definition"), and then turned over again to a special committee — eventually of thirty-five members representing a broad geographical and ideological base — with a finally resulting "consensus definition" of aggression, adopted by the UN General Assembly, without vote, in December 1974. If the Soviet Union hailed this consensus definition as having "accomplished its main purpose of depriving a potential aggressor of the possibility of using juridical loopholes and pretexts to unleash aggression," the distinguished Australian jurist Julius Stone, in contrast, suggested:

> ... that remarkable text rather appears to have codified into itself (and in some respects extended) all the main "juridical loopholes and pretexts to unleash aggression" available under pre-existing international law, as modified by the UN Charter.

Professor Stone further concluded that "the central provisions of this 'consensus definition' are ... an agreement on phrases with no agreement as to their meaning."

Granted all this, why did it take so long? Part of the explanation lies in special, historically-based Soviet approaches to the definition of aggression — the so-called "priority question" — and the Soviet insistence, stemming from (both Soviet and Imperial) Russia's traditional slowness in mobilizing its armed forces in an emergency, that the aggressor in an international conflict must be that state which *first* declares war against another state; or invades that other state's territory without declaration of war; or bombards its territory or knowingly attacks its naval or air forces; or lands its forces in that other state without its government's permission; or establishes a naval blockade of its coast or ports. In the end, and to meet US objections stemming from desires to preserve the option of a preemptive military strike against an opponent visibly prepared to strike itself, at the most favourable opportunity — what, in the aftermath of the Cuban missile crisis, various American jurists categorized as "anticipatory preventive self-defence" — a compromise formulation was achieved and embodied in the UN "consensus definition" of 1974. Under this compromise, the *first* use of armed force by a state in contravention of the UN Charter is to constitute *prima facie* evidence of an act of aggression, with the Security Council, however, specifically empowered to conclude that the determination that an act of aggression has been committed is not justified in the light of other relevant circumstances, including the gravity of the acts concerned.

The UN General Assembly-based "consensus definition" of aggression must be treated, of course, in the light of the larger principles of détente — including, especially, the cold war ground rules or "rules of the game." The Soviet Union established, without any really serious or effective Western protest at the time or thereafter, its own special Moscow (Brezhnev) Doctrine following the events of the "springtime of Prague" and the disaffection of the then Czechoslovak Government within the Warsaw Pact. The Soviet Union and other Warsaw Pact military forces moved into Czechoslovakia on the night of 20-21 August 1968, deposed the Dubcek government, and replaced it with an orthodox Communist régime. This event, closely paralleling the events of October 1956 in Hungary (when Soviet troops entered in strength to displace the transitional government headed by Imré Nagy) — in both the fact of the Soviet military incursion into a Warsaw Pact country against the will of its existing government, and in the absence of any sustained Western protest — led to the enunciation of a number of special principles of socialist (intra-Soviet bloc) international law. These included the notion of collective self-defence of the socialist countries as a whole as legally authorizing intervention by the collectivity (the Warsaw Pact countries) in the affairs of any one member-country; the special Marxist-Leninist principle of sovereignty and the right to self-determination as involving the responsibility of each member-country of the Warsaw Pact not merely to its own people but to all the other countries; and, finally, a general principle of socialist fraternalism and the relations of the socialist states, *inter se*, as transforming into a general (non-national) problem that must be the concern of all socialist countries, a situation "when internal and external forces, inimical to socialism, seek to influence the development of a socialist country with the aim of restoring the capitalist system."

The conservative, "Holy Alliance" aspects of East-West détente, reflected in the Brezhnev Doctrine and seemingly confirmed by conscious Western governmental inaction or by limitation to essentially verbal protests, was apparently echoed in the so-called Sonnenfeldt Doctrine, formulated by the State Department in late 1975 and posited upon the notion of a "natural and organic" relationship between the Soviet Union and Eastern Europe that does not rest solely upon power. In truth, détente from the beginning has always proceeded from cold war realities: the fact of the two great political-military alliances, and the mutual restraint concerning the internal (intra-bloc) problems of the other side; the dependent "spheres of influence" which, if not formally part of either alliance, have a special political relationship to one or other of them because of their military-strategic or other importance, creating a correlative duty of non-interference on the part of the rival bloc. We thus see, together, the two faces of détente. Part of the price of the general reduction of world tensions and the risk of a nuclear or general war is an acceptance of a certain status quo in intra-bloc relations and also in bloc relations with "client" or otherwise politically dependent states. The contradiction between any such artificial jelling of the post-1945, political-military settlement in Europe and elsewhere, and the more general "winds of change" in the world community, is one of the reasons for the decline of détente at the moment of its apparently greatest political success, when its main objectives had been largely consummated or were at least well on the way to achievement.

7 FROM PEACEFUL COEXISTENCE TO ACTIVE INTERNATIONAL COOPERATION?

New Frontiers for Science and Technology

The doctrine of "peaceful coexistence" was the *leitmotiv* of Soviet foreign policy after the de-Stalinization campaign officially began in 1956, when Premier Khrushchev assumed political leadership in the Soviet Union. In his address to the 22nd Congress of the Communist Party on 17 October 1961, Premier Khrushchev assured his audience of top-level, Soviet decision makers that the principles of peaceful coexistence, which he attributed to Lenin, had "always been the central feature of Soviet foreign policy." Premier Khrushchev coupled his remarks on peaceful coexistence with a call for more extensive business relations with all countries, including Britain, France, Italy, West Germany, and other West European countries. Peaceful coexistence and peaceful economic competition, as identified by Premier Khrushchev, were thus firmly linked as the two major elements in the post-Stalin, Soviet diplomatic and political offensive in the West and in the neutralist third world. Apart from its significance in what might be called the polemics of Soviet-Western relations during the Khrushchev era, the subject of peaceful coexistence had been on the agenda and had also been extensively debated at all the biennial reunions, since 1956, of the International Law Association — a worldwide, scientific association of international lawyers that had managed to transcend the ideological frontiers of the communist and capitalist blocs. Beyond this, the United Nations General Assembly included peaceful coexistence on its agenda at its seventeenth session in the fall of 1962, albeit under the somewhat inelegant, Western-sponsored euphemism "friendly relations and cooperation among states." Under this same title, peaceful coexistence was debated exhaustively at every regular session of the UN General Assembly thereafter. In December 1963, friendly relations (coexistence) was given the UN's official *imprimatur* and institutionalized with the creation, pursuant to a General Assembly resolution, of a twenty-seven country (later thirty-one country) Special Committee charged with the "progressive development and codification" of what were essentially the original four principles specified in the Soviet Union's list of principles of peaceful coexistence.

In terms of the internal workings of the United Nations and its specialized committees and agencies, the debate over friendly relations (coexistence) could hardly have come at a better time. In 1960-61, when the matter was initiated in the Sixth (Legal) Committee of the General Assembly, that Committee had very little to do. The prestigious International Law Commission, which it was the nominal responsibility of the Sixth Committee to oversee, was fully occupied with the necessarily slow codification of highly technical areas like the law of the sea, and diplomatic and consular relations. There was a certain natural impatience on the part of the "new" countries with these more traditional processes of progressive development of law; joined with the Soviet bloc pressures for codification of peaceful coexistence, this gave a certain momentum to the work of the General Assembly's Special Committee, which was directed to the elaboration of the detailed, concrete, secondary principles that alone could give meaning to the abstract generality of the concept of coexistence.

It must be noted that, even in Soviet juristic thinking, peaceful coexistence always had a somewhat ambivalent character. Thus, in January 1961, some months before his address to the 22nd Congress of the Communist Party, Premier Khrushchev explained the policy of peaceful coexistence to a Soviet audience as being no more than a "form of intensive economic, political and ideological struggle of the proletariat against the aggressive forces of imperialism in the international arena." Here, Premier Khrushchev may have been appealing to that hard-line, neo-Stalinist remnant of Soviet juristic thinking that would use peaceful coexistence as no more than a convenient camouflage for achieving "proletarian internationalism" in the special sense of coordinated world revolution — in effect, using it as a sort of "Trojan horse" to lull Western suspicions while the Soviet Union proceeded quietly with preparations (again, in one of Premier Khrushchev's colourful phrases) "to bury the West."

In its development in Premier Khrushchev's own personal thinking, however, as evidenced in the empirical record of Soviet foreign policy-in-action, peaceful coexistence increasingly took on the aspect of a somewhat static, even reactionary doctrine — redolent of Metternich and the post-Congress of Vienna "Holy Alliance" attempts to stifle political liberalism and political change in the name of "legitimacy." In effect, Soviet foreign policy in this era became increasingly interested in the possibility, by bilateral arrangements or understandings with the West, of consecrating the political and military balance of power in the world as a formal juridical condition. For peaceful coexistence, in this sense, would amount to a virtual legitimation of the political and military *status quo* of the cold war era. Insofar as it would accept the factual cold war division of the world into the two great military blocs dominated by the Soviet Union and the United States, it would necessarily concede general control and responsibility by each bloc leader over its own sphere of influence. It would further proclaim a principle of non-interference by either the Soviet Union or the United States in the other's bloc, however great the temptation to profit by the other side's difficulties, and however great the moral anguish at not being able to intervene in specific cases. We had this demonstrated most dramatically, as far as the West was concerned, in the frustrations of the West's own, self-imposed restraint in the Berlin and East German riots of 1953, and in the events in Hungary in the fall of 1956. By the same token, Premier Khrushchev must have experienced some of the West's bitter frustration over Berlin and Hungary in the circumstances surrounding the Soviet Union's withdrawal in the fall of 1962 — once President Kennedy had responded resolutely — from its Cuban adventure. This is what was meant, in the somewhat cynical cold war vernacular of the time, by a Soviet-Western understanding to "balance" Hungary and Cuba.

There was a significant development in Soviet-Western "friendly relations" in the years following the peaceful resolution of the Cuban missile crisis. While the standard Western interpretation of the Soviet approach to "peaceful coexistence" had once been the hard-line interpretation, by the middle 1960s it was fairly generally accepted among Western jurists that a working détente had developed between the Soviet Union and the West, and that it was worthwhile to take part in its further elaboration and concretization. Looking back, it may now seem surprising that issues of nomenclature and the quarrel over peaceful coexistence *versus* friendly relations as the preferred legal "term of art" could loom so large in the mutually cautious approach to East-West détente. Writing to the author a few years after those bitter debates over words, Lord McNair remarked how the term "peaceful coexistence," once anathema to Western foreign ministries, had begun to lose its controversial quality. Part of the credit for this change must go to Western lawyers — particularly the "legal laymen," the university professors and practising lawyers outside the various national foreign ministries' specialized legal departments — who refused to be constrained by traditional official positions. In the various professional and scientific arenas for interaction between Soviet and Western lawyers in the late 1950s and early 1960s, Western lawyers pressed their Soviet counterparts to be specific, and to discuss actual problem-situations; it was not enough to talk of coexistence in cloudy generalities. Western lawyers suggested that the Soviet-Western legal dialogue could only be conducted usefully by eschewing bitter and largely futile debate over political ideology, and concentrating on current tensions in Soviet-Western relations together with the immediate range of practical solutions. Here was the genesis of that step-by-step approach to Soviet-Western conflicts that was to be so strikingly vindicated a year later, by its direct employment to achieve the Moscow Partial Test Ban Treaty of August 1963. This same scientific method was accepted in a quiet, *de facto* manner by Soviet jurists (including the then Principal Legal Adviser to the Soviet Foreign Ministry, the very able and balanced Professor Gregory Tunkin), in place of the old-line, *a priori*, absolutist approach that had stressed the resolution of Soviet-Western conflicts through one comprehensive, law-making act that set out a universal, general code of principles of peaceful coexistence. Their acceptance for the first time really permitted cooperative, Soviet-Western scientific effort towards the ending of the cold war and the relief of international tensions in practical ways.

The emphasis on concrete problem solving, and the practical breakthrough achieved by replacing ideological debate with empirical methods, call attention to the fact that in the more technical, scientific areas, Soviet-Western cooperation (or at least recognition of common interests) had always been present — even before the political détente of Premier Khrushchev and President Kennedy. We might even say that the most promising route to genuine Soviet-Western cooperation, transcending the somewhat negative condition of coexistence inaugurated by political détente, is through the approach to technical, scientific problems. For here the record suggests that the more demanding and difficult the problem, in scientific terms, the greater Soviet and Western reciprocity of interest is likely to be. It is the scientists themselves (construing this term in the broadest sense to include social scientists) who are best equipped, on both sides, to secure fundamental Soviet-Western understandings in these areas, since they are less bothered by the ideological preconceptions and *a priori* moral judgments that have generally so preoccupied or frustrated professional diplomats in the past.

This proposition can be illustrated by the substantial practical success of Soviet-Western scientific problem solving in concrete cases. We can examine and assess the record shortly. In the meantime, it is worth nothing that the problem-solving approach carries its own internal momentum, and at a certain point lends itself to the induction of general principles on a thoroughly empirical basis. In contrast the essentially *a priori* approach, with its emphasis on abstract principles, will often lag badly behind actual problem-situations and get caught up in largely sterile ideological debates. The UN Special Committee on Friendly Relations, after the first enthusiastic response from Soviet bloc and third world countries following its formation in 1963, ran into seemingly endless difficulties in rendering precise and operational what was, in essence, a set of rather vague propositions replete with semantic confusions. Then, something rather strange began to occur. The original proponent of formal codification of peaceful coexistence, the Soviet Union, seemed to lose interest in the work of the Special Committee as Soviet differences with the West were resolved in concrete cases. As Soviet involvement in the Special Committee seemed to decline, Western foreign ministries could hardly see the need for continuing Western response. The Committee's labours continued, however. The main political initiatives and the intellectual dynamism were supplied by jurists from politically more neutral, "middle" countries or from the third world. Some of these, like Milan Bartos of Yugoslavia, saw in the friendly relations exercise not simply a convenient vehicle for détente for the two bloc leaders, but also a juridical device which, imaginatively used, could help the cause of self-determination and pluralism within the blocs. "Why not coexistence inside the blocs?" asked the Yugoslavs. By the same token, imaginative third world jurists like Krishna Rao of India saw in the elaboration and extension of the principles of friendly relations (coexistence) the practical possibility of protecting non-aligned, neutralist countries from big power "hegemony" — whether Soviet, or American, or even that joint (Soviet and American) condominium form of hegemony that seemed presaged as differences shaded off between the two bloc leaders.

The Special Committee finally completed its task in 1970, and its work is recorded in the Declaration on Principles of International Law concerning Friendly Relations and Cooperation among States in accordance with the Charter of the United Nations, embodied in a UN General Assembly resolution of October 1970. The Declaration enshrines seven principles, which can be briefly summarized as follows:

1. The duty of states to refrain from the threat or use of force against the territorial integrity or political independence of any state;
2. The duty of states to settle their international disputes by peaceful means;
3. The duty not to intervene in matters within the domestic jurisdiction of any state;
4. The duty of states to cooperate with one another;
5. The principle of equal rights and self-determination of peoples;
6. The principle of sovereign equality of states;
7. The duty of states to fulfil in good faith the obligations assumed by them in accordance with the Charter.

What did it all achieve? On first sight, the Declaration seems as abstract — some might unkindly say, as vacuous — as the original Soviet list of principles of peaceful coexistence from which it emerged a decade and a half later. An American delegate, unconsciously reflecting Southey's musings on the Battle of Blenheim that it was, after all, "a famous victory," publicly hailed it as "one of the major achievements of the Twenty-Fifth Anniversary of the United Nations." He suggested that in his own and other countries' foreign ministries, legal advisers' perceptions of the issues had been "clarified and sharpened" in the whole process. That, perhaps, is the key. When the Declaration was finally achieved in 1970, it had become a somewhat irrelevant footnote to historical changes long since established by more prosaic, essentially problem-oriented methods. But the *process* of negotiation between East and West (with some interesting neutralist and third world input, particularly towards the end), that lasted over a decade and was necessarily conducted in an intellectually disciplined way in yet another institutionalized international arena, may have helped in softening rival doctrinal positions that had been taken too categorically in the first place. In the end, détente was achieved progressively and empirically, prior to and without the necessity of the formalized Declaration of 1970.

To return to the problem-oriented approach with emphasis, now, on the area of science and technology, we may consider the quite substantial practical achievements in Soviet-Western cooperation — in highly technical areas demanding high technical skills — at times when, at a more strictly political level, further progress in ameliorating Soviet-Western relations might not have seemed very promising.

First, the problem of the peaceful exploration and development of Antarctica. The United States Department of State, realizing the danger of international conflict caused by the welter of rival national claims in Antarctica, had taken the diplomatic initiative in 1948 and proposed to the countries then having competing claims to territorial sovereignty in Antarctica — Argentina, Chile, France, Norway, Great Britain, Australia and New Zealand — the desirability of calling an international conference looking towards possible internationalization of Antarctica. The reaction of the seven states, however, was generally hostile to any surrender of national claims, and so the matter had to be dropped. At this stage, the Soviet Union came into the picture for the first time, demanding full participation in any Antarctic settlement. The US State Department had not, of course, included the Soviet Union in its list of interested states — 1948 being the year, by most counts, of the inception of the cold war. Following the Soviet bid, matters were allowed to drift for some years, though India proposed the question of Antarctica for discussion at the UN General Assembly in the fall of 1956.

The maturing of plans for International Geophysical Year brought Antarctica back as a subject for international scientific discussion, however, and also brought full-scale Soviet involvement. International Geophysical Year (1958), or IGY, was planned and administered by a special committee of the International Council of Scientific Unions. Though in some countries, particularly those of the Soviet bloc, scientific societies and academies are wholly or partly government controlled, the emphasis of the Council has been so clearly scientific that in the view of competent Western observers, it has been able to preserve a relatively independent, non-governmental character. The Antarctic figured prominently in the Council's programme for IGY right from the outset. Regional conferences on the Antarctic, in connection with IGY, were held from 1955 onwards, with the Soviet Union sending official delegates and taking a leading part throughout.

There was genuine concern, at the time, that the cold war might be extended to the South Pole, particularly since the Soviet Union had been assigned base sites and IGY responsibilities in the territorial sector of Antarctica claimed by Australia. During this period, governments were being urged from many sides to take steps to assure their own national claims in Antarctica; at the same time, there remained the countervailing scientifically based interests in maintaining freedom of inquiry in the Antarctic continent. The IGY, in this sense, was a scientist-conceived and scientist-developed programme, operating under the clear understanding of all the scientists from the various national groups — Soviet bloc, Western, and "uncommitted" — that all activities conducted during IGY would be politically neutral in the sense of involving absolutely no ruling, one way or another, on the legal character of existing claims to territorial sovereignty in Antarctica. While it clearly would have been possible, *legally*, to conclude a final settlement of the political status of Antarctica prior to the Soviet participation in IGY, limited to Western countries that alone had international law-based territorial claims in that region, any such agreement was *politically* impossible because of the welter of competing Western claims and the mutual intransigence of those same Western countries in what was, after all, a non-cold war issue. After Soviet participation in IGY, any future Antarctic régime that would exclude the Soviet Union had clearly become politically, if not indeed legally, impossible.

The next political moves concerning Antarctica were clearly designed to build upon the era of inter-systems good feeling that had permeated the multinational effort in Antarctica during IGY. Some months prior to the termination of IGY, President Eisenhower foreshadowed a dramatically new approach to regulation of the Antarctic continent. In the American President's own words:

> The United States is dedicated to the principle that the vast uninhabited wastes of Antarctica shall be used only for peaceful purposes. We do not want Antarctica to become an object of political conflict. . . .

We propose that Antarctica shall be open to all nations to conduct scientific or other peaceful activities there. We also propose that joint administrative arrangements be worked out. . . .

President Eisenhower then proceeded to invite a group of twelve countries including all existing territorial claimants to Antarctica, plus the Soviet Union, and finally also Japan (which had itself formally renounced any territorial pretensions to Antarctica in the World War II Peace Treaty of 1951), to take part in an international conference in Washington designed to permit a direct transition from IGY to a new international régime in Antarctica. Some fifteen months of discussions then ensued, characterized by the same inter-systems cooperation that had been so notable throughout IGY. The chief Soviet delegate, Mr. Kuznetsov, expressed from the outset the Soviet Union's interest in settling the régime for Antarctica on an international basis. The final outcome of the conference was the Antarctic Treaty, signed in Washington on 1 December 1959.

The preamble to the new treaty expressly noted both the "substantial contributions to scientific knowledge resulting from international cooperation in scientific investigation in Antarctica," and the "establishment of a firm foundation for the continuation and development of such cooperation on the basis of freedom of scientific investigation in Antarctica as applied during the International Geophysical Year."

The key operational provisions of the Antarctic Treaty of 1959, for present purposes, are Articles 1, 3, 5 and 7. Article 1 provided:

> Antarctica shall be used for peaceful purposes only. There shall be prohibited, *inter alia*, any measures of a military nature, such as the establishment of military bases and fortifications, the carrying out of military manoeuvres, as well as the testing of any type of weapons.

Article 5, in the same spirit (and anticipating by four years the Moscow Partial Test Ban Treaty of 1963), declared:

> Any nuclear explosions in Antarctica and the disposal there of radioactive waste material shall be prohibited.

It was in Article 3 of the treaty, however, that the positive spirit of international, scientific cooperation, so successfully established in International Geophysical Year, was captured and extended. Article 3 provided for the exchange of information regarding plans for scientific programmes in Antarctica; for the exchange of scientific personnel between different national expeditions and stations in Antarctica; and for the exchange of scientific observations and the results of scientific investigation and research. This was concretely followed up in Article 7, which provided for the designation of national observers, with authority to carry out detailed inspections of all areas of Antartica, including all stations, installations and equipment, and all ships and aircraft. Article 7, which also permitted aerial observations, was designed to ensure the proper carrying out of the provisions of the treaty.

It remains to say that the Antarctic Treaty remains in full operation to this day, without any serious complaint as to violation of its terms or essential spirit. The patterns of concrete, Soviet-Western cooperation in a technical, scientific area where Soviet and Western long-range interests were essentially the same, were followed four years later in the successful Soviet-Western negotiations leading to the conclusion of the Moscow Test Ban Treaty of August 1963. We have already discussed the Moscow Test Ban Treaty above. It is only necessary to note, in passing, that while the Khrushchev-Kennedy détente may have provided the political opportunity for discussing the banning of nuclear weapon tests, it was the weight of scientific evidence on both sides concerning their danger to human life that succeeded in communicating a special sense of urgency to the political leaders' attempt to reach a firm Soviet-Western agreement. The common danger that acknowledged no ideological frontier, and was amply attested to by scientists from both main ideological systems, thus led inevitably to common acceptance of the control of nuclear weapon testing in the form of a firm international legal accord resting on the inter-systems consensus.

The Moscow Test Ban Treaty of August 1963 had dealt tangentially with the peaceful regulation of outer space, insofar as its ban on nuclear weapon testing extended to outer space. In January 1967, agreement was finally reached on a comprehensive treaty governing the peaceful regulation of outer space and space exploration. The text of the treaty had been worked out in the United Nations Committee on the Peaceful Uses of Outer Space, and in its expert legal subcommittee headed by Polish jurist Manfred Lachs.

The immediate negotiations leading to the treaty lasted almost six months at the United Nations. They had been preceded by years of difficulty, and by protracted and seemingly fruitless discussions between lawyers and scientific experts from the Soviet Union, the United States, and other countries. Agreement, however, had become certain — barring, of course, any major unexpected political development marring Soviet-United States relations, such as a marked or unexpected step-up in American military involvement in Vietnam — in June 1966 when, within a day of each other, first the Soviet Union and then the United States filed with the Secretary-General of the United Nations almost identical texts for a draft treaty on space. The Soviet version was for a treaty "On principles governing the activities of States in the exploration and use of Outer Space, the Moon, and other Celestial Bodies," while the American version was for a treaty "governing the exploration of the Moon and other Celestial Bodies."

The final text, as approved by the UN Committee and then, formally, by the UN General Assembly, declared in its opening Article:

> The exploration and use of Outer Space, including the moon and other celestial bodies, shall be carried out for the benefit and in the interests of all countries, irrespective of their degree of economic or scientific development.

The same article went on to affirm: "Outer Space, including the moon and other celestial bodies, shall be free for exploration and use by all states without discrimination of any kind," and that "there shall be free access to all areas of celestial bodies," and "freedom of scientific investigation in Outer Space."

The main operative provisions of the new treaty were contained, however, in two articles. Article 2 proclaimed:

> Outer Space, including the moon and other celestial bodies, is not subject to national appropriation by claim of sovereignty, by means of use or occupation, or by any other means.

Article 4 read as follows:

> States/parties to the treaty undertake not to place in orbit around the earth any objects carrying nuclear weapons or any other kinds of weapons of mass destruction, install such weapons on celestial bodies, or station such weapons in Outer Space in any other manner.

The same article went on to declare that "the moon and other celestial bodies shall be used . . . exclusively for peaceful purposes," and that "the establishment of military bases" and "the testing of any type of weapons" was forbidden (though the "use of military personnel for scientific research or for any other peaceful purposes" was not).

When one looks at Articles 2 and 4 — the principal constructive achievement of the new space treaty — one must acknowledge that the new treaty probably did not break much legal ground. The orbiting of nuclear weapons in space vehicles, for example, was expressly prohibited by the United Nations General Assembly resolution of 17 October 1963, which had originally been passed with joint Soviet and American backing. This had been one of the fruits of the Khrushchev-Kennedy détente highlighted by the successful signing of the Moscow Nuclear Test Ban Treaty in August 1963. Though some formalistic lawyers might still deny the effect of law to a UN General Assembly resolution even where it rested, as here, on the consensus of the main competing political and social world systems, most of the world community had accepted the resolution on non-orbiting of nuclear weapons as binding international law from the moment of its adoption in the United Nations. And, of course, this particular principle was fully observed — in the spirit and in the letter — in the more than three years between its first adoption in the UN General Assembly resolution and its final incorporation in the Outer Space Treaty in January 1967.

As for the notion that the moon and other celestial bodies should not be subject to national appropriation or national sovereignty, that principle had been expressly conceded by Soviet international lawyers, both in the Soviet-Western discussions at the authoritative, if private, International Law Association, and in Soviet scientific legal writings on space. The Soviet opinions on this issue were all the more interesting because first advanced at a time when the Soviet Union had a head start on the West in space explorations; it therefore seemed likely that the Soviet Union might try to apply customary international law rules governing territorial ownership and title, to the moon at least.

In the end, perhaps, the importance of the Outer Space Treaty of 1967 lay not so much in any legal novelty of the principles finally expressed in treaty form, as in its indication of two political realities. First, the achievement of a firm treaty on outer space confirmed what had been apparent to students of Soviet-Western relations over a number of years, namely, that in matters of a highly scientific character where the Soviet

Union and the United States had achieved approximately the same level of technical development, it was not too difficult to record these facts in a formal agreement resting firmly upon mutuality and reciprocity of interests between the Soviet and American systems. Hence, for example, the Moscow Test Ban Treaty of August 1963; hence, also, the original 1959 agreement on Antarctica, providing for its non-military use and for scientific cooperation in its exploration.

The second and most significant reason for the importance of the Outer Space Treaty of 1967 was that it represented the first really substantial breakthrough, of a publicly acknowledged character, in Soviet-Western relations after the Moscow Test Ban Treaty of August 1963 and the United Nations General Assembly resolution on non-orbiting of nuclear weapons in space vehicles of October 1963.

The high hopes engendered by both these measures for a step-by-step progression to further concretization of the Khrushchev-Kennedy détente were shattered by President Kennedy's assassination in Dallas in November 1963, and by Premier Khrushchev's abrupt dismissal from office the following year. The next three years were rather bleak from the viewpoint of formal inter-systems accords going to fundamental issues of conflict, as new and apparently less sympathetic individuals than Khrushchev and Kennedy came to power in the Soviet Union and the United States. The Outer Space Treaty re-established the rhythm of inter-bloc accommodation between the leadership of the two main countries, leading in turn to the Nixon-Brezhnev détente and the Moscow "Summit" Accords of May 1972.

The progressive achievement of big power détente and the new era of scientific and technological cooperation seemingly inaugurated by the Antarctic Treaty of 1959 and the Outer Space Treaty of 1967, at first seemed to offer the prospect of a new international law of communications, particularly where it concerned the regulation and development of telecommunication satellites and telecommunication satellite broadcasting. The necessarily very high technological component of discussions limited effective participants, in the early stages certainly, to the Soviet Union and the United States. The technical-scientific establishments in these countries had attained a level of professional expertise, confidence, and articulateness that allowed them to influence national policy making in ways hardly possible in other areas of East-West interaction, which were seemingly more open to and more readily comprehensible by lay decision makers. The legal specialists or legal technocrats, in their consummate professionalism, had dominated this area of Soviet-Western relations from the beginning at the expense of the legal generalists or legal laymen. But this, in turn, created some unexpected difficulties when political-ideological problems — involving difficult policy choices that might normally have been foreign to a highly technical area in which the main protagonists had relative parity — intruded into the debate. While the antinomy of policy and function is of course present in other areas of international legal negotiation, the conflict between the two approaches, and between the generalists and the specialists sponsoring them, was more noticeable than ever in the approach to a new international law of communications. This was undoubtedly one of the factors inhibiting the development of a genuinely intersystemic, common law in spite of all the objective factors that seemed to favour a substantial and far-reaching Soviet-US accommodation in this area.

There is not, of course, any tidy blueprint for the international law of communications — no single constitutional document for a common international agency, setting out the institutional bases for international organization and international decision making in the field, as well as the main substantive legal principles or at least philosophical guidelines for their development and application. This is a direct consequence of the historical fact that the international law of communications did not emerge poetically, as the United Nations Organization did in 1945 with its brand new and purportedly all-encompassing fundamental charter, but more or less *ad hoc*, over the years. It developed in response to problem-situations in the area of telecommunications and international broadcasting that seemed to demand not so much inter-national as trans-national solution or regulation. Its prime emphasis has been on functionalism. The resultant institutional structure has been particularly closely correlated with the technical-scientific needs of the individual problems being solved, and technical-scientific considerations have tended to dominate the process of decision making.

This explains why, when the use of space and space satellites for international broadcasting became both technically and commercially feasible, the first international control and development initiatives were *not* entrusted to the long-established, specialist, international agency already existing in the telecommunications field — the International Telecommunication Union (ITU) — but to an entirely new organization specially developed on an *ad hoc* basis for the purpose (INTELSAT). While the ITU certainly had a high degree of specialist expertise within the general telecommunications field, it was an expertise limited essentially to posts, telegraphs, and telephones; at that time it did not include space technology. In addition, its specialized, international bureaucratic cadre had been recruited mainly from national posts and telegraph personnel. When the new problem of international utilization of space communications arose, therefore, the general consensus was that the ITU simply would not do. Hence the decision to form the completely new international agency, INTELSAT.

But where the progress of disarmament was controlled by the major arms developers (the two superpowers), international telecommunications and its international regulation tended to be shaped from the outset by the prime space utilizer (the United States), which dominated the telecommunications field in terms of scientific knowledge, trained personnel, and the enormous capital required, at least initially, for its development. At the time of the Interim Agreements of August 1964, under which INTELSAT was formed, the post-cold war détente between the Soviet Union and the United States was still in its very early stages; moreover, there was a certain time lag between the Soviet Union and the United States in the telecommunications field. When INTELSAT emerged, therefore, under the August 1964 agreements, it was possible to argue that it was not only politically inevitable but also necessary for effective telecommunications development, that the United States should assume both majority voting control in the new INTELSAT international organization, and effective management control through the United States' domestic common carrier for profit, COMSAT. These two key elements in INTELSAT — the weighted voting in the international agency, and the use of a particular national agency as its executive component — were often strongly criticized in the years immediately after 1964. Weighted voting in an international agency is not, of course, unprecedented, for it also exists in the International Monetary Fund (IMF), in the UN Conference on Trade and Development (UNCTAD), in the International Coffee Agreement, and arguably even in the UN Security Council itself, with the built-in veto of big power, permanent members. Indeed, it might be suggested that the principle of weighted voting, with effective decision-making power linked to financial or other relevant input, has become almost a norm in areas where the demands of functionalism are especially high, and where problem-solving competence demands special contributions, in terms of finance and skills, from certain countries.

The criticisms of INTELSAT usually looked to questions of degree rather than to questions of kind: the effective voting veto given to the United States, with its 53 percent financial investment in the INTELSAT system; the inevitable conflict of interests where the US Government agency COMSAT wore "three hats" at the same time — as a US domestic, common carrier for profit, as US national representative to INTELSAT, and finally as the general managerial authority within INTELSAT itself. The most serious indictment of INTELSAT, however, was that, as a functions-oriented, international organization established in the post-cold war era of détente, it did not include the Soviet Union — which had, of course, a significant presence of its own in space communications. The responding argument would have to be that the United States had never barred the Soviet Union's entry into INTELSAT, and that the US majority voting interest was hardly beyond renegotiation and possible downgrading in the event of a Soviet bid to join. Be that as it may, no direct Soviet initiative to join INTELSAT emerged. Instead, the Soviet Union proceeded to operate its own regional organization — INTERSPUTNIK, directed to the Communist countries — separate from, and in potential rivalry to, INTELSAT. The 1964 Interim Agreements on INTELSAT were eventually replaced, in 1971-72, by new Definitive Agreements that finally approved the phasing out of the US, COMSAT-based, management rôle over a six-year period, and also provided for the reduction of US majority voting control to a maximum of 40 percent in the new Board of Governors for INTELSAT. It is possible that these measures, introduced in timely fashion as early as 1964, might have overcome Soviet reservations about the supposedly universal character of INTELSAT. By 1972, however, when the Definitive Agreements were finally ratified, it was too late. The two parallel organizations, INTELSAT and INTERSPUTNIK, were already firmly established, and any common principles in the new international law of communications would have had to be reached bilaterally, in negotiation between the two rival organizations. The failure to achieve a common, international organization is the sadder because, of all areas of potential East-West cooperation, communications seemed objectively to be among the most promising, given its scientific-technological component and the advanced academic training of its key participants. This failure had important consequences that carried over from the strictly technical, functional areas to policy areas, where speech and communication interests seemed to conflict with national security and protection of national identity and culture. The Soviet Union, facing the problem of accidental or deliberate spillover of satellite television broadcasts from one country to another, sought express prohibition in treaty form — with a Draft Convention on Principles governing the use by States of Artificial Earth Satellites for Direct Television Broadcasting, submitted to the UN Outer Space Committee and then to the UN General Assembly itself — of "any material publicizing ideas of war, militarism, Nazism, national and racial hatred and enmity between peoples, as well as material which is immoral or instigating in nature or is otherwise aimed at interfering in the domestic affairs or foreign policy of other States."

A basic antinomy existed between the US, commercial television-influenced, "open society" approach to satellite television broadcasting and its regulation, and the more traditional, "protection of state sovereignty," "non-intervention in the internal affairs of states" approach of the Soviet Union. This conflict was reinforced by a quickly-emerging third world position concerned with the maintenance of indigenous civilizations, cultures, ways of life, languages, and religions against alien, materialistic, and predominantly Western intrusions through television broadcasts spilling over from one country to another without the prior permission of the receiving country. The antimony is a real one, and the conflict of social interests that it reflects can hardly be solved on an absolutist, either/or basis. It seems to call out, rather, for the kind of compromise based on mutual reasonableness and reciprocity of interest, that characterized big power détente in its early, concrete realizations. In the absence of a common institutional forum where such accommodations could be developed through the application of pragmatic, empirical methods to concrete problem-situations, the resolution of this antimony has been made only slowly and conservatively — perhaps, in the result, favouring "content control" at the expense of the more liberal, "open society" values.

8 THE "WINDS OF CHANGE" IN THE WORLD COMMUNITY

The Quest for a New International Economic Order

In the 1964 edition of what was then the main Soviet textbook on international law — edited by Professor Kozhevnikov who was himself, very briefly, the Soviet judge on the World Court — Western conceptions of the nature and basic character of international law were severely criticized. As the Soviet textbook contended:

> The bourgeois juristic science limited itself, as a rule, only to formal dogmatic definitions of international law. It is not in a condition to reveal its essence, class nature and social purpose in the contemporary epoch.

We in the West would certainly not be disposed to agree with the conclusion of Professor Kozhevnikov and his colleagues, that it is only possible to explain the essence of contemporary international law on the basis of Marxist-Leninist principles. Nevertheless, intellectual candour does compel us to admit that — as one of the more intellectually imaginative of the post-World War II American jurists, Myres McDougal, complained — too much of Western international legal science has been devoted to an "over-emphasis on technical rules unrelated to policies as factors in guiding and shaping decisions." The old-line Western legal theories looked not to the substantive policy content of a claimed rule of law, but to the various formal categories of official sources of international law to which it might be allocated. In a word, the fundamental inquiry for deciding whether a claimed rule really deserved the accolade of being called international law was not what was in it (meaning whether, intrinsically, it was a sensible or fair rule), but where it came from (meaning whether it was custom, treaty, or the like).

Many Western lawyers have been trained in positivistic theories of law; law is viewed, in Austinian terms, as being command, without regard to its moral content as such. One can understand that, for these jurists, identifying the "source" of a claimed rule may be enough to complete the process of inquiry into whether it really is international law. In addition, these same jurists come from national legal systems that actively participated in the historical formation of rules of customary international law; and their nations tended to dominate the actual negotiation and elaboration of treaty-based international law in the key historical periods of large-scale treaty making. Their countries' national self-interest was thus fully consulted, as it was certainly fully represented, in the creation or definition of those same rules.

Yet this is hardly true for the "new" countries that succeeded to independence and self-government upon the collapse of the old colonial empires in Asia and Africa, or for the post-1918 "succession states" that came into being after the downfall of the old imperial dynasties in Central and Eastern Europe. For these countries, the crucial question is likely to be whether a claimed rule of international law is a good rule or a bad rule — to be ascertained by the extent to which the claimed rule maximizes the various competing interests being pressed in the world community. In this context, the argument from age alone is hardly likely to be very persuasive. Age, by itself, is surely neutral, for one used to burn witches under the authority of the positive law. Mr. Justice Oliver Wendell Holmes, Jr., of the United States Supreme Court, used to say it was revolting to have no more substantial justification for a claimed legal rule than that it was so laid down in the time of Henry IV. Perhaps this same philosophy is represented by the comment of Soviet jurist Professor Gregory Tunkin on the extent to which the "new" Afro-Asian countries are bound by old rules of customary international law created before they came into political existence. Professor Tunkin's own suggestion is that any rule of international law based on "custom" must satisfy the double standard of being satisfactorily evidenced through historical practice of states, and of being actually "accepted" by states. Professor Tunkin thus makes the agreement of states — inter-systems consensus — the essence of the creation of norms of international law.

Does this mean that all claimed principles of international law must be subjected to a sort of international "rule of reason" before they can be admitted as normative and binding at the present day? There was a time, perhaps, when Soviet jurists seemed bent on rejecting the whole corpus of traditional or classical international law — or at least pre-1917 international law — as *per se* outdated and without juridical effect. Yet any fears of legal anarchy in the world community must be tempered by a consideration of more modern Soviet juristic writings. Western international lawyers, remembering with Mr. Justice Oliver Wendell Holmes, Jr. that the life of the law has not been logic but experience, would certainly approve of Professor Tunkin's later statement that the "science of law, like all other sciences, must base itself on facts, the facts of international life." Again, we could hardly do less than welcome Professor Tunkin's public recognition of the continuing juridical viability of "old democratic fundamental principles of international law." The overall trend of Professor Tunkin's latter-day, academic writings is, in fact, a skilfully attempted approximation of Soviet international law thinking to more generally accepted, orthodox or classical doctrine. When Professor Tunkin joined issue in public with Sir Francis Vallat, the Legal Adviser to the British Foreign Office, for example, it was to insist that he was advocating "new international law" only, and that he certainly had called "neither for 'a new international law' nor for a 'revolution' in international law." And so, Professor Tunkin took great pains to stress that Soviet jurists have "no intention of overthrowing the international law now in force."

It seems to me that what Professor Tunkin was saying here — and he was still speaking as the Principal Legal Adviser to the Soviet Foreign Ministry, prior to his election as Professor Korovin's successor in the Chair of International Law at Moscow — was that the need today is for a more or less evolutionary international law making. This would accept the existing corpus of classical international law as the necessary starting point for legal innovation and for the creative adaptation of old rules and principles to new political, social, and economic conditions in the world community. Such a juridical approach has, of course, a very great deal in common with some Western-based intellectual attitudes, stemming from the legal realist and sociological schools of thinking. These would eschew old-fashioned, positivistic, law-as-command approaches to law in favour of detailed, empirically-based study of the *de facto* claims and interests being pressed, and would also accept a positive law as changing as society and its component interests change. On this approach, the most remarkable feature of international law immediately following the Khrushchev-Kennedy détente was the demonstration, again and again, of common, Soviet bloc and Western interests in so many of its rules and principles. For very many, if not the great bulk, of the principles of "classical" international law continued to be viable, since they rested on clear mutuality of interest between Soviet and Western systems.

To explain this startling fact, given the fiery polemics of the Soviet-Western debate during the cold war years, is to recognize several important truths. First, the acceptance of a pragmatic, empirical, step-by-step approach to resolution of Soviet-Western conflicts meant a replacement of the erstwhile *a priori* absolutism on both sides in favour of scientific problem solving. The very de-ideologization of the conflict facilitated common solutions, since it allowed attention to focus on the actual problem and the range of alternative solutions, unfettered by rival philosophical preconceptions or by cold war propaganda in general. But the very de-ideologization of the Soviet-Western conflict, and the growing awareness that both sides would tend to identify the really significant problems in the same way and reach the same essential conclusions about the best solutions, were themselves a consequence of marked social and economic advances in the Soviet Union up to that time; of the increasing approximation of Soviet industrial strength and economic production to Western levels; and of the progressive *embourgeoisement* not merely of the actual Soviet decision-making cadre but also of managerial and technocratic personnel and the intelligentsia in general. (Societies at relatively similar stages of social and economic development tend to share the same general problems and employ the same social controls or legal remedies to resolve them — whether according to scientific Marxism in its modern empirical form, as represented by the new generation of Soviet jurists, or according to Western-based sociological jurisprudence.) It was hardly surprising, then, that the Soviet Union should become increasingly concerned with more traditional legal values: historical continuity; predictability in legal development; and due deference to settled expectations of the sort that any mature legal system, whether in the international or national arena, is supposed to protect. It was hardly surprising, again, that in the same new empirical spirit Professor Tunkin should charge Soviet jurists, using language oddly reminiscent of the American legal realists, with "weakness and incompleteness in juridical argumentation and a tendency to slip into the easier path of ready-made political argumentation reinforced by quotations." He charged them with "dogmatism . . . the use of citations instead of creative thought . . . isolation from actual reality."

Professor Tunkin went on to state that the main goal for the new, post-Stalin, post-cold war, Soviet science of international law was not merely "knowledge of what exists in international law but active participation in changing it."

Soviet international law, in this new period of maturity, was certainly empirical and problem-oriented. But at the same time it was inevitably concerned with recognizing and assisting widespread social change in the world community. When the younger Soviet jurist, Professor R. A. Touzmoukhamedov — who taught international law at that special university set up in Moscow for students from the "new" Afro-Asian countries, the Patrice Lumumba Friendship University — contended that the "wars of national liberation" did not contradict the principles of Soviet-Western friendly relations (peaceful coexistence), and that the UN General Assembly, by adopting the Universal Declaration of Human Rights, gave a form of *de facto* standing to national liberation movements, he served notice that the Soviet Union had no intention, in spite of continually extending détente with the West, of giving up its earlier psychological warfare and material support on behalf of decolonization, national independence, and self-determination. Concrete Soviet follow-up to such abstract principles, in terms of arms and *matériel* and "volunteers," would of course be conditioned by power realities and the dangers of escalation into big power conflict and nuclear war. But the principles themselves could hardly be abandoned by Soviet decision makers without intolerable loss of face in the third world, and without further Chinese Communist charges of Soviet ideological "revisionism." Soviet juridical science could thus be expected to maintain an ambivalent, Janus-like attitude, looking forward to the Soviet Union's assured future as one of the politically great and economically prosperous, industrial civilizations, and at times backward to its original, revolutionary, Marxist heritage.

The intellectual dilemma of latter-day Soviet jurists is the problem of reconciling their obligations of deference to original, abstract, *a priori*, Marxist legal principles with the pragmatic exigencies of contemporary Soviet foreign policy. However, there were other, earlier contradictions, especially the dichotomy between economic base and legal superstructure, in Soviet legal theory as applied to international law.

Since law is, in classical Marxist legal terms, a product of the marketplace, and each economic system thus gets the body of law appropriate to its stage of economic development, how can two different economic systems, capitalism and communism, yield identical bodies of international law doctrine? Putting it in more traditional Marxist language, if international law, like national law, belongs to the superstructure and is uniquely determined by the base of productive relationships, how can radically different (capitalist and communist) economic bases yield the same superstructure of international law?

The great Soviet jurist of the late 1920s and early 1930s, Pashukanis, tried to resolve the dilemma in 1935 with an asserted antinomy between *form* and *content* in law: although the forms of international law might be identical for all states, opposing social systems could use these legal forms for their own ends. After Pashukanis's downfall in 1937 before Stalinist orthodoxy and the new, ultra-positivist legal notions developed as its main instruments, other Soviet jurists entered the fray. Professor Eugene Korovin described the "common" international law, applying to both capitalist and communist legal systems, as simply "identical norms of various legal superstructures." Professor Tunkin, while rejecting Professor Korovin's "heresies," offered the Soviet Union's own catalogue of principles of peaceful coexistence as the scientific-legal rationalization of the substantial and continually expanding area of Soviet-Western legal consensus and legal common interest — reflected in the emerging international law of détente and going to nuclear disarmament, arms control generally, security of territorial frontiers, and scientific and technical cooperation and economic exchange between the two blocs.

A Western-trained legal sociologist might explain the phenomenon somewhat differently. It is clearly true that "classical" international law stems essentially from Western political societies founded on the rise of commerce, and that its main substantive principles were developed in the liberal phase of Western civilization and Western constitutionalism. If this body of law reveals itself as more and more acceptable to Soviet jurists today, because more and more responsive to the needs of Soviet foreign policy in action, it is because of the historical transformation of Soviet society and the changes in its economic base and decision-making élite, so that these correspond, more and more, to Western society. It is not for nothing that big power détente is increasingly seen by many third world countries as a purely artificial, legal construct, masking a substantial accommodation — of basic interests and outlook, and preferred expectations as to the future development of the world community — long since achieved, quietly and *de facto*, between the two superpowers. These third world countries see détente as a form of big power condominium, rather like that approved world public order system decreed by the Congress of Vienna for post-1815 Europe in the name of Metternichean "legitimacy" and effectively maintained by the Concert of Europe and "Holy Alliance" system. It is not for nothing that contemporary People's Republic of China jurists identify "imperialism" today in terms of two manifestations — capitalist imperialism and social imperialism — and that, for them, big power hegemony represents the operation of one or other of these two, more or less arbitrarily and interchangeably, but always adversely to basic third world interests. This particular, "Chinese," aspect of the intellectual debate over the nature of international law draws attention to the fact that, for third world countries at least, the relation between economic infrastructure and legal superstructure has taken on a prime importance once again. On this argument, it is only by building a new, more genuinely democratic and inclusive world economic system that one will attain a new, more genuinely democratic and inclusive international law and thus transform the "old," "classical," Western-based system. Change the economic system and you will change the legal system; however, insofar as law and society operate together in a symbiotic relationship, imaginative and forward-looking innovations in the positive law can, if made in a timely fashion and before the political situation in the world community has become pathological and out-of-hand, facilitate progress towards a more equitable economic order. Here, in any case, lies the intellectual genesis of the third world-based campaign, in the United Nations and other international arenas, for a new international economic order.

The sharp welling of Afro-Asian resentment over the World Court majority decision in July 1966 in the *South West Africa* case, is another reminder that the sharpest divisions of the last part of the century are not between the Soviet bloc and the West, but between the highly industrialized, technologically advanced, affluent countries — which include both the United

States and its main allies, and the Soviet Union and its European associates — and the remaining, economically underprivileged countries of the world. The old East-West (Soviet-Western) conflicts of the cold war era, as President de Gaulle was the first among Western political leaders to recognize, have increasingly been replaced by a new North-South geographical division corresponding to differences in standards of living and in general economic and physical well-being.

It is becoming clear that the achievement of a viable system of world public order, during the last part of the century, depends in large measure on narrowing this gap. At present, the disparity between the economically privileged and underprivileged countries is constantly increasing, because of the extraordinary technological advances that continue to be made in the former group.

Recognition of the common, Soviet-Western interest in promoting economic and social development through strengthened bilateral and multilateral cooperation, was decisive in launching the United Nations Decade of Development. President Kennedy, in his speech to the UN General Assembly on 25 September 1961, rightly recognized that economic development could become a cooperative, Soviet bloc *and* Western enterprise. The UN General Assembly responded to President Kennedy's appeal at its sixteenth session by designating the 1960s as the Development Decade, with an official target for 1970 of a minimum annual growth of 5 percent in the national incomes of the less developed countries, to be achieved through United Nations-sponsored technical assistance, regional surveys, pilot projects, and other programmes for promoting economic growth.

One very concrete, institutionally-based, United Nations effort for achieving this was the United Nations Conference on Trade and Development or UNCTAD, as it came to be known by trade officials around the world. UNCTAD was called into being by the United Nations Economic and Social Council at the initiative of the less developed countries, who laid the groundwork for it in meetings of UN regional commissions and special committees in Latin America, Asia, and Africa. In a Joint Declaration of seventy-seven developing countries, made at the conclusion of the UNCTAD conference in June 1964, the conference itself was described as a "significant step towards creating a new and just world economic order."

The central purpose of UNCTAD was to consider ways of bridging the so-called Prebisch Gap, named after the conference's own Secretary-General. This was the gap between the foreign exchange the developing countries would need to finance their import requirements for development, and the foreign exchange they were likely to earn from their export of primary goods. UNCTAD Secretary-General Prebisch himself, however, estimated that by 1970 this gap would reach 20 billion dollars per year, assuming imports sufficient to support the 5 percent annual growth target laid down by the United Nations General Assembly. And even if half this gap could be filled by foreign aid, it would still, according to Dr. Prebisch's estimate, have left about 10 billion dollars to be financed through increased exports by the less developed countries.

UNCTAD itself provided a clear confrontation between the rich, predominantly white states of the northern hemisphere (both Soviet bloc and Western), and the poorer, predominantly non-white states of the southern hemisphere. For the first time, a really coherent and organized developing countries' lobby appeared, comprising the originally seventy-five and later seventy-seven Latin American, Asian, and African countries represented at the conference. The seventy-seven caucused together and chose to negotiate through common spokesmen. They also voted as a bloc in order to pressure the industrialized nations. UNCTAD was thus the first major international conference in which the conventional East-West, Soviet-Western confrontation that had characterized international relations throughout the cold war era, was replaced by the new North-South alignment.

The sheer weight of numbers of the seventy-seven developing countries caused fears on the part of the minority, northern states that resolutions might be forced through without regard to the feelings of this minority, which would, after all, inevitably be called on to bear the main economic burdens of the majority decisions and recommendations. The Western countries had originally promoted a forty-member Trade and Development Board, responsible to the UN General Assembly, with fourteen Western seats (ten permanent) and with a collective veto. The final conclusion of the conference, however, was in favour of a fifty-five member Board, with eighteen seats for the West, twenty-two for the Afro-Asian countries, nine for Latin America, and six for the Soviet bloc, and with voting by simple majority. In general, the UNCTAD proposals and recommendations called on industrial countries to impose a moratorium on trade barriers to the main commodity exports of developing countries, to reduce internal taxes, and to broaden quotas.

It would be easy to say that UNCTAD and the UN Decade of Development provided both the goals and a structural base for a more equitable world economic order. The fact is, however, that the UN resolution inaugurating the Decade of Development set an exceedingly modest goal in looking to a 5 percent accrual of national income in the developing countries by 1970. As the leading Czech jurist Professor Rudolf Bystricky pointed out, this meant 100 dollars per capita per annum at most — by all standards, a minimal individual income. Dr. Bystricky's own solution for helping to bridge the gap between the privileged and underprivileged countries, was to require the former colonial powers to pay financial compensation to their former territories. As Professor Bystricky explained, such an obligation of compensation would be imposed upon the former colonial powers "for the exploitation and depradation of their natural wealths, for the immense losses caused by the deformation of their economies, and for the plunging of the populations of the former colonial nations into unheard-of misery."

Professor Bystricky drew upon his own considerable reputation as a Marxist theorist and international lawyer to urge that such a duty of financial compensation existed as a legal obligation under international law itself. Dr. Bystricky was also highly critical of the final decisions of the United Nations Conference on Trade and Development of 1964, blaming the fact that "no universal autonomous organization for international trade was created but only an auxiliary organ of the General Assembly" on the proposal of weighted voting made by the Western states at the conference, allegedly in the fear that they might be outvoted by the overwhelming numbers of developing countries.

While the remedy advanced by Professor Bystricky might seem as politically drastic as it was certainly (in international law terms) novel, it is doubtful whether it would really have been too significant in bridging the economic gap between the developing countries and the advanced industrial states, even if it had been adopted. Nor could the tentative steps taken by UNCTAD and the Decade of Development be regarded as much more than a promising beginning. And so that "margin of misery" between rich and poor countries continued as perhaps the major problem of world public order of the last part of the century.

It was eminently reasonable by the late 1960s, as Soviet-Western détente progressively unfolded, to expect that peaceful coexistence might lead to active international cooperation between the two blocs, permitting joint, Soviet-Western programmes for massive economic development assistance to underprivileged countries. This hope was soon dashed by the political events of the 1970s, without doubt the most disappointing decade of the post-war era. We have already touched sufficiently upon those events: the apparent disappearance of societal consensus within the United States on main foreign policy objectives, as political dissension grew in the last years of the Vietnam War; and the concomitant lack of public confidence in the American ideal and the American mission abroad. These problems were compounded by the Watergate crisis and the subsequent weakening of presidential executive power. Doubts as to American leadership and its constancy of purpose, abroad, produced cracks in the Western military alliance and inevitably affected that Soviet-American balance or understanding on which détente itself rested. These problems of Western, intra-bloc and Soviet-Western inter-bloc relationships were compounded during the Carter presidency by the image of a frequently irresolute or vacillating executive in the United States. This executive allowed the American armed strength that was a precondition of effective big power détente to decline, and alternated unpredictably between a hard-line, pragmatist-realist approach to international law and relations, and a vaguer, largely intuitive form of natural law. Perhaps it is not surprising that, facing the evident decline in Soviet-Western relations and the apparent lack of meaningful Soviet or Western economic initiatives to redress the marked North-South imbalance, key third world countries and regional groupings began to turn to direct political action.

Among the initiatives available to the third world were "direct action" in its various forms: political terrorism; internal subversion; aid to popular revolutionary movements abroad; collective voting strength where it could be mobilized in the United Nations and other specialized agencies, and in specialized, multilateral conferences like the marathon Law of the Sea Conference; and finally, cartel-like, regional or group, pressures in economic matters where particular third world countries had a monopoly or near-monopoly in the supply or production of scarce natural resources. Such direct action was not uniformly successful, of course, and it operated with differing degrees of intensity and persuasiveness depending on the particular arena and technique, the individual actors, and the intrinsic importance of the substantive issue concerned. Then again, by the accident of their colonial heritages, the third world countries were more richly endowed in legal than in economic talent and training. As a result, they may have tended to exaggerate the importance of largely hortatory legal resolutions or declarations at the expense of more concrete, if low-level, economic measures and economic problem solving. We can illustrate this proposition by looking at some of these third world-based political initiatives towards a truly new, international economic order.

First, in the area of "direct action" in the strict sense of the word, political terrorism had already emerged by the middle 1960s as a revived mode of correcting injustices of the existing world public order system, quickly and forcefully. It was seen as an alternative to the ordinary political processes and constitutional channels of the United Nations General Assembly, the World Court, and conventional diplomatic negotiation *inter partes*, which offered no effective solution at all or a very tardy and partial one. The sporadic and usually individual attacks on crowned monarchs and other heads of state at the end of the nineteenth century — largely symbolic manifestations of the anarchist movements of that era — led, eventually, to two abortive League of Nations exercises in the late 1930s after the assassination of King Alexander of Yugoslavia and French Foreign Minister Barthou in 1934: a convention on the prevention of terrorism; and a convention for the creation of an international criminal court with jurisdiction over political terrorists. These conventions occupied the old League of Nations for three years but never came into force, perhaps as much because of their absurdly limited range of legal concern, the protection of heads of state, as the novelty (for the 1930s) of attempting to create an effective international criminal jurisdiction.

It was not until the 1960s, however, that political terrorism really emerged as a rationally conceived, concerted plan of action for large-scale political and social change where clogs effectively existed — or more importantly, perhaps, were perceived as existing — in the mechanisms for orderly change through the ordinary, constitutional-legal processes of the United Nations and other official decision-making arenas. The spearhead of the organized terrorist revival at that time was the Palestine Liberation Organization. Through recourse to such direct action, it claimed to exercise the right to self-determination of the Palestinian people in the West Bank, Jordanian region, and in other territories, like the Gaza Strip, occupied by Israeli military forces since the 1967 Arab-Israeli War. Its immediate weapon was the illegal diversion and capture by armed force (the "hijacking") of civil aircraft of the airline companies of major Western countries.

The example had already been set by the sporadic actions of individual, often "lunatic fringe" characters in the early 1960s who, after publicly proclaiming their support for Castro's Cuba or other romantic, left-of-centre, political causes, succeeded in embarrassing the US State Department and harassing US airlines by forcibly diverting civil aircraft from their normal destinations to Havana. For the Palestine Liberation Organization the advantages of adopting the same technique, but on a much more rigorously organized basis, seemed to lie in instant, worldwide, media attention for a political cause whose fortunes were faring badly in the official United Nations arenas through failure to secure any form of legal recognition or official admission to UN conclaves. The immediate disruption of international civil air transportation was considerable, as were the immediate publicity gains for the PLO and its cause. But the politically counterproductive aspects of aerial piracy were also very soon apparent and the PLO, seeking increasingly to "legitimate" its operations, perceptibly changed course and turned to more conventional forms of political action. At the same time, the world community in its politically organized form moved to legislate against the new evil of aerial piracy. Three major new international conventions — the Tokyo Convention of 1963, the Hague Convention of 1970, and the Montreal Convention of 1971 — were sponsored by the United Nations and its specialized agency, the International Civil Aviation Organization. The record of actual performance under these multilateral treaties is disappointing; there is an unfortunate gap between the number of states signing the treaties, the number going on to ratify the treaties, and the number finally taking concrete steps to implement the treaties in their own internal law. Nevertheless, these official gestures at the international level pointed the way to quieter measures at the national level, which effectively solved the aerial piracy problem for most practical purposes: on-the-ground police surveillance; pre-flight screening of all aircraft passengers and their baggage; and airport terminal security checks. When instituted on a systematic and scientific basis from the early 1970s onwards, these measures virtually eliminated aerial piracy and hijacking attempts in the United States and other main airline countries following its lead. This was accomplished without any significant inconvenience, delay, or financial cost to airline companies, their air crews, or their passengers. It is a principle of international law, no less than of municipal, national law, to exhaust the lesser, more modest forms of social control before escalating to more sweeping measures. There was a public educational value, to be sure, in the three great aerial piracy conventions already referred to, but one wonders why it took the major air transportation countries and their national airlines so long, and why they were so reluctant, to introduce the relatively modest, but in the end amazingly successful, national legal-administrative controls that finally solved the problem.

The task of international legal problem solving, in the area of terrorism and direct political action, is to maximize the advantages of ordinary political processes for the actors, while at the same time minimizing (by effective preventive and control measures, as in the aerial piracy example) any political gains to be made by these extraordinary, extra-legal means. If quick and far-reaching solutions on substantive issues like a Palestinian "homeland" cannot realistically be expected through the United Nations proper because of the big power veto in the Security Council, and procedural hurdles in the General Assembly, one should not underestimate the opportunities for significant, incremental progress through the UN committee and specialized agency structure, and through diplomatic negotiation *inter partes* as an originally revolutionary movement becomes increasingly domesticated or legitimated within the UN community. Most third world countries, and even some Western countries, have their own national, revolutionary traditions; key Afro-Asian leaders were once legally proscribed in their home countries as political terrorists. This may explain the reluctance to legally ratify, or actively implement international conventions directed against the use of terrorist methods, even on such self-evidently worthwhile and politically non-controversial subjects as the Prevention and Punishment of Crimes against Internationally Protected Persons, including Diplomatic Agents — the subject of a convention adopted in New York in December 1973.

UN General Assembly Resolution 34/145, adopted on 17 December 1979, attempted to resolve the inherent contradiction in the world community's necessary disapproval of acts that endanger innocent lives through hostage taking, indiscriminate attacks, and the like, and the UN General Assembly's new commitment to self-determination, independence, and national liberation movements directed against what the resolution terms "colonial and racist régimes and other forms of alien domination." The verbal accommodation was achieved in a resolution entitled "Measures to prevent international terrorism which endangers or takes innocent human lives or jeopardizes fundamental freedoms, and study of the underlying causes of those forms of terrorism and acts of violence which lie in misery, frustration, grievance and despair and which cause some people to sacrifice human lives, including their own, in an attempt to effect radical changes." But the actual UN General Assembly vote adopting the resolution, 118 to 0, had 22 abstentions including the United States, Great Britain, France, West Germany, Japan, Canada, and Israel. Even within that regional grouping of states resting upon basically homogeneous cultural, political, and legal values, Western Europe, the Council of Europe-sponsored, European Convention on the Suppression of Terrorism adopted in November 1976, and the somewhat smaller, European Communities-sponsored, Agreement concerning the Application of the European Convention on the Suppression of Terrorism among the Member States adopted in December 1979, were achieved only by conceding a "political offences" exception to the general state obligation to extradite terrorists for trial by another contracting state.

If terrorism and related forms of direct action now seem downgraded as counterproductive by organized political groups that are increasingly becoming "legitimated" from an earlier "national liberation movement" status, there is no doubt of the political results to be obtained by marshalling the third world voting majority in the UN General Assembly, UN specialized agencies, and diplomatic conferences organized under UN auspices for the elaboration and adoption of multilateral treaties of a designedly law-making character. The precondition to such political success, in UN arenas, is of course that the third world voting bloc remain united and monolithic. This presupposes, in turn, a continued coincidence of the main third world countries' national interests in specific problem areas and on specific voting issues.

When the creation of a new international economic order has been approached through its postulation in legislative form — by legislative *fiat*, so to speak — it has indeed proved possible to marshal the third world voting majority in the UN General Assembly in an impressive display of group solidarity and common purpose. Thus, the first two General Assembly resolutions proclaiming, in programmatic form, the new economic system — the Declaration on the Establishment of a New International Economic Order, and the so-called Programme of Action on the Establishment of a New International Economic Order — were adopted without vote at the General Assembly's sixth special session on 1 May 1974. The final element in this triad of law-making ventures, the Charter of Economic Rights and Duties of States, was adopted by the General Assembly at its twenty-ninth regular session on 12 December 1974 by a recorded vote of 120 to 6, with 10 abstentions.

There had been some confusion at the General Assembly's sixth special session over the rôle of a voting consensus, for the United States and some other Western countries had insisted upon filing express "reservations" to the Declaration and to the Programme of Action in spite of the seemingly unanimous consensus behind the "without vote" adoption in each case. The third world majority, annoyed with these Western reservations, was not disposed to compromise over the December 1974 Charter, and the Western countries, annoyed in their turn with what they considered to be third world intransigence, decided to vote against the Charter or to abstain. This explains the six negative votes, which included the United States, Great Britain, and West Germany, and the ten abstentions, which included France, Italy, Japan, Canada, and Israel.

The Charter itself, though perhaps not atypical of General Assembly ventures into law making, still leaves a great deal to be desired in its conception and styling. On the one hand, it followed what may be called the cornucopia approach to legal drafting: when in doubt, throw everything in and leave it to subsequent historians to work out why. It also embraces what has historically been characterized as the Weimar Constitution drafting principle: if faced with latent or even patent contradictions in demands pressed in the drafting stage, put them all in and hope that the passage of time will resolve the antinomy by disposing of one or other alternative. Thus, the Charter proclaims state sovereignty in its most unrestrained form, in its opening articles.

> Article 1. Every State has the sovereign and inalienable right to choose its economic system as well as its political, social and cultural systems in accordance with the will of its people, without outside interference, coercion or threat in any form whatsoever.
> Article 2. (1) Every State has and shall freely exercise full permanent sovereignty, including possession, use and disposal, over all its wealth, natural resources and economic activities.
> (2) Each State has the right:
> (a) To regulate and exercise authority over foreign investment within its national jurisdiction in accordance with its laws and regulations and in conformity with its national objectives and priorities . . . .
> (b) To regulate and supervise the activities of trans-

> national corporations within its national jurisdiction and take measures to ensure that such activities comply with its laws, rules and regulations and conform with its economic and social policies. . . .
>
> (c) To nationalize, expropriate or transfer ownership of foreign property, in which case appropriate compensation should be paid by the State adopting such measures, taking into account its relevant laws and regulations and all circumstances that the State considers pertinent. . . .

But the Charter goes on to apply stern injunctions against any one state's attempt to limit or influence another state through economic measures.

> Article 16. (2) No State has the right to promote or encourage investments that may constitute an obstacle to the liberation of a territory occupied by force.
>
> Article 18. . . . In the conduct of international economic relations the developed countries should endeavour to avoid measures having a negative effect on the development of the national economies of the developing countries, as promoted by generalized tariff preferences and other generally agreed differential measures in their favour.
>
> Article 32. No State may use or encourage the use of economic, political or any other type of measures to coerce another state in order to obtain from it the subordination of the exercise of its sovereign rights.

Some parts of the Charter are general, rhetorical proclamations, as with the pronouncement on the elimination of apartheid.

> Article 16. (1) It is the right and duty of all States, individually and collectively, to eliminate colonialism, *apartheid*, racial discrimination, neo-colonialism and all forms of foreign aggression, occupation and domination, and the economic and social consequences thereof, as a prerequisite for development. . . .

Other parts of the Charter are the new, "socialist" international law of the late 1950s and the early 1960s, with a postulated duty of the advanced industrial states to make restitution and compensation to other states.

> Article 16. (1) . . . States which practise such coercive policies [i.e., colonialism . . .] are economically responsible to the countries, territories and peoples affected for the restitution and full

compensation for the exploitation and depletion of, and damages to, the natural and all other resources of those countries, territories and peoples. It is the duty of all States to extend assistance to them. . . .

There are specific articles on the law of the sea and on environmental policy.

> Article 29. The sea-bed and ocean floor and the subsoil thereof, beyond the limits of national jurisdiction, as well as the resources of the area, are the common heritage of mankind. . . .
>
> Article 30. The protection, preservation and enhancement of the environment for the present and future generations is the responsibility of all States. . . .

The range is wide; the coverage is diffuse. The lack of strong intellectual discipline in the drafting of the Charter, and in the establishment of criteria of relevance, in the end leave the impression that the Charter is largely hortatory, that it is nominal and not normative. And so the question arises, What is to make the new Charter operational, in terms of concrete economic relations between the developed and developing countries in future? In the strictly economic domain, is there any reason to assume that the enactment of the Charter, in UN General Assembly resolution form, has effectively established its programme as the dominant model for a new, economically-based, world public order system?

The pressures successfully applied by the OPEC cartel after October 1973, for massive increases in world market prices of crude oil, demonstrated the first real solidarity among third world countries in the use of their control of raw materials as an economic weapon. It may also have given developing countries a real sense of political power in the world community for the first time. Yet, paradoxically, the oil price increases exaggerated differences between third world countries because of those countries' extremely divergent growth rates. No such moves could occur without innocent victims, and the victims — those most affected by the oil price increases — were very poor already.

The Western industrial countries may have provided some help, for instance through the Oil Facility of the IMF, but they clearly preferred to favour their own affected group within the OECD. The OPEC countries also came to the aid of the poorer countries, but they applied their own system of grading according to special cultural links; they seem to have given assistance first to Arab countries, thereafter to Muslim countries, and only latterly to all others.

What the crisis over oil prices served to demonstrate, in fact, was the degree and depth of the current split within the third world itself. For there is, by now, a "new" third world, comprising all those third world countries possessing important raw materials or a fully competitive industrial sector or else (most fortunate of all) both raw materials and a competitive industrial sector. These third world countries — mainly East Asian, Middle Eastern, and Latin American, and including only a few African countries — amount by now to the world's "middle class." Most of them have achieved high growth rates while the Western industrialized countries have gone through a period of severe economic recession. By contrast, there is within the third world bloc a group of the really poor nations of the world — most southern Asian countries, most African countries, and the smaller Latin American states — which now can be called the "fourth" world. The enormous increases in grain, crude oil, and fertilizer prices, and the repercussions of the recession in the West, have thrown these fourth world countries into a crisis that threatens to undermine all international and regional development aid projects. The very divergence of interests and disparity of basic economic resources within the third world raise, in fact, quite as many prospects for disintegration of the bloc in future as for the maintenance of that solidarity against the industrialized countries that was demonstrated so strikingly during the international oil prices crisis. Provided, of course, that the "new" third world is prepared to exercise generosity towards the fourth world, the united front on economic issues should remain unbroken. The fourth world has strongly attacked the "economic strangulation" of the poorer countries through higher oil prices, but this action has seemingly been intended to put pressure on the producing countries within the third world bloc as a whole to help the non-producers in their ranks through special oil prices and massive investment.

Related to both the *legislative* initiatives of third world countries towards a new international economic system, and the *economic cartel* pressures exercised by them through the OPEC group (which, it must be remembered, is not confined to the Arab oil-producing states but includes key representatives from other regions like Venezuela and Nigeria), is the concerted action successfully mounted in specialized international diplomatic conferences held under United Nations auspices and directed to the adoption of a multilateral convention as the end product. The best known example is, of course, the Third United Nations Conference on the Law of the Sea, officially launched by a UN General Assembly resolution of December 1970, and coming to resemble the mythical Labours of Sisyphus as it proceeded, throughout the entire decade, from one round of specialized meetings to another with no apparent conclusion. While there were undoubted procedural (adjectival law) defects in its conception and planning that contributed to its sustained failure, there were other, more fundamental problems — for example, the confusion between international legal *codification*, in the strict sense of a (fairly modest) restatement of the existing, largely custom-based law, and a more substantial act of international *law making* or novation, going beyond even that "progressive development" and imaginative restatement inherent in codification and present, for example, in the earlier, 1958 UN Conference on the Law of the Sea. Once you go beyond legal codification and venture upon international law making in the larger sense, the problem changes from one of identifying and concretizing existing rules, to one of either mobilizing sufficient political support behind those already existing rules or changing them altogether where no such support can be found.

The phenomenon of the Third UN Conference on the Law of the Sea was the number and range of states ready to abandon over three centuries of *mare liberum* doctrine in favour of a new species of *mare clausum*, in which more and more areas of the sea, its fishing and marine life stocks, and its submarine mineral resources, were blocked off and appropriated by individual states. Only certain types of states continued to maintain the classical international law concept of the sea: the two superpowers, with large military submarine fleets and interests in maintaining a right of overflight for their military aircraft over as much of the sea as possible; states with large merchant marine fleets and, therefore, a clear and immediate economic interest in preserving existing rights of passage at sea; and states with either no coastal fishing resources of their own, or no continental shelf and hence no offshore mineral and related resources to exploit. These states supported the concept of the sea and its resources as being open to all states, as the "common property of all mankind." The traditional, three-mile territorial sea of "classical" international law gave way to a "patrimonial sea" that often extended as far as two hundred miles out from the low-water line along the coast, and was recognized and enforced by means of interlocking, usually bilateral accords concluded between states sharing the same special economic interests. Even more dramatic in their impact were the claims advanced for control over the continental shelf, the seabed and the ocean floor and their resources. Here a clear conflict emerged between the advanced industrial states that alone had the scientific-technological capacity to exploit the oil, mineral, and other resources involved (and therefore favoured a laissez-faire, open-to-all-comers approach), and the industrially backward nations including, especially, landlocked states or coastal states with no continental shelf and thus no offshore mineral resources of their own to exploit. The latter favoured "internationalizing," in a special *ad hoc* UN control authority, the ownership of the resources concerned, the direction and planning of their mining, and the sharing of financial profits on some generally equitable basis. These rival claims were, in a certain real sense, unbridgeable except by the sort of exercises in reciprocal give-and-take to which the two superpowers had become accustomed in working out détente. Here, however, the two superpowers were not the two opposing key players, for their interests were often complementary, and the number of players was very much greater. This, and the fact that the differences were much more North-South than East-West, in the conventional post-cold war sense, explain the delay throughout the 1970s in reaching substantial consensus on the content of a new law of the sea.

The Law of the Sea Conference had thus become transformed from a mere codification exercise into something more — a case study in the elaboration and application, in one major area of world community activity, of the new economic development law. For very many post-colonial, third world states, the principle of decolonization and independence that had already been successfully applied in the political domain should now be used to achieve economic objectives; this meant, in relation to the law of the sea, rewriting the "classical" régime of the sea, which they saw as the product of an essentially narrow political consensus among those dominant Western societies that had been founded upon the rise of commerce, and as a reflection of their special economic interests.

The widely hailed, diplomatic "breakthrough" at the close of the resumed Law of the Sea Conference sessions in Geneva in July and August of 1980 — chief US negotiator Elliot Richardson suggested that historians would see it as "the most significant single development of the rule of law since the founding of the United Nations itself" — may, in this sense, reflect the heartfelt relief of professional negotiators at having something in documentary, treaty form to show for their years of effort, more than it indicates a genuine and lasting reconciliation between the conflicting economic interests of the third world and the high technology, post-industrial societies of the West and the Communist bloc. The complicated compromise agreement issuing from the 1980 Geneva sessions would effectively split profits from deep seabed and ocean floor mining between the world community, represented by a new International Seabed Authority, and the private mining companies (national and multinational) with the technology capable of conducting such deep seabed and ocean floor operations. The interests of the high technology, post-industrial societies would seemingly be safeguarded by a unique voting formula to be applied in the new International Seabed Authority; a complex, "three-tier" system would separate substantive decisions into three categories, each requiring a different level of agreement (two-thirds, three-fourths, or "consensus") for approval. A final, comprehensive convention enbodying this compromise, as well as earlier agreements on other law of the sea issues, was defined as the goal of still further conference sessions to be held in New York in the spring of 1981 with the final objective of signing the convention in Caracas before the end of 1981.

Decolonization, in its classic, post-World War II political manifestation, approached its consummation in the spring of 1980 with the final achievement of full independence for Zimbabwe (Rhodesia) following a war of national liberation. Only the larger Southern African question remains to be settled. Thus, the *first* phase of the world revolution of our times may be said to have ended, and the *second*, economic phase to have begun. This is often called, in the special language of the times, the struggle against "new colonialism" in the sense of foreign economic exploitation.

The dominant goals of the new international economic order, reversing the "terms of trade" in world trade and reversing the terms of foreign investment by seeking to give developing countries unlimited sovereignty over their own economic resources, have been sought primarily through raw material power with the formation of producers' cartels for each basic raw material. The oil cartel, OPEC, has certainly been spectacularly successful in gaining its objectives, though with some quite unfortunate and presumably unintended side effects within the third world bloc. Similar successes, if not on quite the same scale, have also been achieved with bauxite and with phosphates. Indeed, the attempt to maintain a cartel-style situation in the mining and export of phosphates, and thereby to maintain artificially high prices, seems to have been an inarticulate major premise of the policy positions of several of the key actors — Spain and Morocco, for example — in that otherwise difficult to explain, delayed decolonization drama in the Spanish Sahara in the early 1970s, which was later the subject of a World Court Advisory Opinion in *Western Sahara* in 1975. In the long, post-decolonization war of national liberation, the populist, Polisario forces, backed by the Algerian Government, battled Moroccan and Mauretanian military forces to which Spain had, in a cleverly-planned political deal, ceded control.

Attempts to organize cartels for other major raw materials have not always yielded positive results. Raw material prices have, of course, fallen because of the massive recession in the industrial countries, and so the success of cartels, as an economic weapon of the third world bloc, is not clear. Indeed, the two basic demands made by the third world — raw material cartels, and immunity of foreign investments from the protections of classical international law — seem a hardly sufficient basis for a viable world economic order. The indirect effect of massive increases in raw material prices, as a result of monopolistic controls, has been aggravated inflation and recession in the industrial countries. This has meant correspondingly fewer exports of raw materials from third world countries to industrial countries, higher prices for fertilizers and capital goods exported from industrial countries to the third world, and, in the end, less development aid from Western countries to the third world because of the West's own financial difficulties. The end result has been a loss of growth for the developing countries.

The third world bloc, so long as it retains its cohesion and solidarity, could certainly defeat resolutions of the United Nations General Assembly aimed at achieving such current Western objectives as the introduction of a new international currency system; or such current Western and Soviet objectives as the exploitation of the mineral resources of the sea; or more general, post-industrial society (both Western and Soviet) objectives like the defeat of international terrorism or the control of international drug smuggling. The third world bloc could also, if it stays united, attempt to trade off its needed cooperation in environmental protection and population control against a far more serious commitment on the part of the industrialized countries, both Western and Soviet, to international economic development aid.

But the threat of a negative vote in the United Nations General Assembly could not, of itself, provide a recipe for positive action on the part of the world community as a whole. On the law of the sea, for example, the third world bloc encountered, to its evident surprise, a considerable degree of Soviet bloc and Western solidarity on substantive issues. Beyond that, the Soviet Union appeared even more committed than the West to resisting third world attempts to amend the United Nations Charter so as to reduce big power influence and political control, and to "democratize" the United Nations generally and make its main arenas more responsive to majority will. It is true that third world ventures in international law making have sought their main outlet through multilateral, as distinct from bilateral, action, and that this implies a return to the United Nations, with specialist United Nations committees thus increasingly transformed from technical or expert gatherings to still further arenas for the formulation and development of more general foreign policy objectives: decolonization in vestigial situations like South Africa; elimination of "neocolonialism," loosely defined to cover situations where undue political influence still exists between former colonial powers and their post-independence, "client" states; furtherance of national self-determination in instances not meeting the strict "decolonization" criteria but otherwise qualifying as genuine "national liberation" struggles; and achievement of a truly new (and more democratic and inclusive) international economic system.

Is there, after all, any reason to assume that this postulated new economic system of world public order will replace other more traditional political-juridical models in the near future? In responding to current third world drives for a new international economic order, the West would seem to have a number of different options.

The first option would be to concentrate on one's own self-interest as narrowly conceived, and try to introduce one's own new economic order in the economic triangle of the United States, Western Europe, and Japan, with Western international economic development aid kept close to present, relatively modest levels.

A second clear option would be to concentrate on the key nations of the third world, attempting to reach an understanding with OPEC and the oil-producing nations and with a few of the other major raw material producers. Such a strategy, if successful, would certainly separate and isolate the "new" third world from the fourth world, and would mean forgetting altogether about the new international economic order, except insofar as that might be involved in any deal with OPEC and other major raw material producer cartels.

The third and certainly the most positive option would be to set up a new and more inclusive global economic order that would incorporate all the nations of the world, and at the same time to address not only strictly economic problems, but also the new problems arising from interdependence such as environmental deterioration, world population, and food scarcity.

In considering the political possibilities of these options, it may be instructive to look to the historical development after World War II of the movement for decolonization and national self-determination. This movement was originally spearheaded in the General Assembly by the third world countries and did not finally become consummated until the middle 1970s, but by that time it had the widespread and fairly general support of the big powers. This movement inaugurated the main historical trend in international law after World War II, and all countries were eventually caught up in it. Even if it now seems likely that the main Western countries, partly because of third world tactical errors or oratorical excesses, will move cautiously in their response to the current movement for a new international economic order and seek special bilateral deals or trade-offs with the more important producers of raw materials among the third world majority, it is still important to try to understand the "winds of change" in the world community. Enlightened self-interest on the part of the industrialized, Western and Soviet bloc states suggests that the current drives for a new international economic order by the third world bloc should be accepted not merely as confirming the appearance of the new North-South alignment in international relations, but also as heralding the end of an epoch in world public order and the transition to a new one. For, as the Report of the Independent Commission on International Development Issues, headed by ex-Chancellor Willy Brandt of West Germany, noted in 1980: "Whatever their differences and however profound, there is a mutuality of interest between North and South. The fate of both is intimately connected. The search for solutions is not an act of benevolence but a condition of mutual survival."

9 A NEW, PLURALISTIC WORLD LAW AND WORLD ORDER SYSTEM

International Law Antinomies of an Era of Change

We live in an era of transition from an old system of world public order to a new one whose exact contours and directions are not yet clearly or firmly established. What is certain is that, as President de Gaulle predicted in the mid-1960s, the postwar era is coming to a close or has already ended. This era included both the long, drawn-out period of the cold war and the system of bipolarity resting on the Soviet and American military blocs, and the subsequent period of big power interaction and accommodation that Soviet and Western jurists identified as peaceful coexistence or friendly relations and later called détente, and that third world jurists, especially the Chinese, might more soberly and dispassionately call big power condominium or "hegemony."

In retrospect, it seems possible to say that the threat of East-West nuclear war may never have been quite as serious as it seemed to be during the cold war. To be sure, the period was characterized by constant testing and probing, on both sides and by both big powers, of points of weakness or indeterminacy in those border areas that had not been clearly defined as belonging in one of their "spheres of influence" in the relatively hasty preparation of the political-territorial blueprints for the postwar world during the Allied heads of state conferences of 1943-1945, and at the war's actual end in Europe in the summer of 1945. What is truly remarkable is that the basic political configuration of the world community has hardly changed at all — at least in Soviet-Western terms — since the Big Three's grand design at the Yalta Conference of February 1945, which was ratified by the Potsdam Conference of August 1945. Everything that has happened since has confirmed a basically conservative pattern of evolution within the world community, viewed from the Soviet-Western perspective, with the prime emphasis on defence of vested interests and the political-military status quo of 1945, in spite of the occasional excesses of cold war rhetoric on both sides and the talk, for example, of "overthrowing imperialist lackeys" or "rolling back communist imperialism."

The fault, if fault is to be found in all of this, must be traced to its historical roots at Yalta in February 1945, and to the Allied leaders who so casually, and with frequent disregard of historical and sociological facts, cast lots for the high and the low, and disposed of other peoples' destinies as well as their own — often without even paying lip-service to the principle of self-determination. Yet, in terms of the ultimate survival of the world community, big power détente or condominium did not perform so badly as the basic ordering principle for international relations for the three decades that followed the war's end. It kept the peace, by and large, and it successfully contained the threat of big power nuclear conflict. The historical judgement on that particular era in international relations must rest on comparisons with other, similar periods after similar great military conflicts. For example, during the Concert of Europe or the "Holy Alliance" following the Congress of Vienna in 1815, big power peace was maintained for almost a century, albeit at the price of political orthodoxy and attempts to restrain fundamental political, social, and economic change in the name of the principle of legitimacy.

It seems certain that the era of big power détente or condominium would have come to an end of its own accord, even without the casual factors of personality and executive leadership on both sides that characterized the latter part of the 1970s. Revived propaganda battles simply reflected changes in the world community that the big powers were as unable to comprehend fully as they were unable to control. The drastic weakening of American executive leadership in reaction to presidential excesses during the Vietnam conflict, and the sharp decline in America's will to continue acting as "policeman of the world," simply accelerated a process already under way because of objective, historical forces extrinsic to the United

A NEW WORLD ORDER SYSTEM

States itself. The political restiveness within each of the blocs, and the dissatisfaction with the consequences of a monolithic foreign and economic policy seen to be determined ultimately by the two superpowers, created centrifugal tendencies within each of the blocs that would surely have led to their ultimate dissolution with the increasing flow of goods and services, trade and commerce and technology, and — finally — cultural and political ideas across political-military frontiers. The ill-conceived and clumsily executed propaganda campaigns that were launched in the late 1970s against the advice of supporting bloc members were, on this view, politically counterproductive in terms of their concrete results, and historically retrograde in that they delayed or defeated liberalizing forces already in motion. But, beyond all that, the increasingly vocal and self-confident countries outside the two blocs began to oppose a world public order system which they saw as denying them effective participation in key decision making, and which they also saw as an instrument for maintaining a political and economic status quo inimical to their own long-range self-interest. This opposition engendered a challenge from third world countries to big power détente or condominium, and to the world public order system on which it was posited.

Developing new models of a world public order system in scientific-legal terms requires extrapolation of long-range trends and conditions in the world community. This is an especially difficult task since one is fixed in an era of transition, which is inevitably beset by conflicting social forces that sometimes lead in diametrically opposed directions. Instead of being able to identify common goal values for a new public order system based on common objectives of the world community for the future, one is very often left with a series of (in Radbruch's terms) legal *antinomies*: alternative, sometimes parallel and sometimes competing approaches, on which no firm, pluralistic consensus has yet emerged in an increasingly plural world community. Disagreement as to goal values is often accompanied by disagreement as to the process (governmental institutions and techniques) for implementing those values, insofar as particular institutions or processes — judicial settlement of disputes, for example — are sometimes viewed as being rooted in particular ethno-cultural or legal value-systems and so loading the final solutions. What we may be left with, therefore, is the need to establish alternative developmental constructs — possible sequences of events running from a selected cross-section of the past, through the present, to the future — in order to clarify and facilitate the choice among the antinomies and the adoption of concrete techniques for achieving them.

One such developmental construct might be that the trend away from bipolarity has proceeded so far that it is beyond redemption, even with revived interest on the part of the big powers in renewing and extending détente; thus, the present tendency to political fragmentation and dissonance within the world community will continue. This might mean polypolarity, lack of co-ordination and cohesion in key world community policy making, and a correspondingly greater risk of irrationality and capriciousness on key decisions concerning the recourse to armed force, or the containment or avoidance of nuclear war.

Another, much more optimistic developmental construct would be that while bipolarity and big power condominium are clearly in decline because of historical forces beyond the control of the key actors, the transition will be an orderly one, staged and assisted by the big powers themselves; thus, we would move fairly gracefully and easily into a new, more genuinely pluralistic world community.

What is clear, however, is that alternative constructs based on world domination by only one of the two superpowers — either a *pax americana*, vitiated when the Soviet Union developed its own nuclear weapons in the late 1940s and discarded for quite pragmatic reasons along with John Foster Dulles's largely verbal crusade for "rolling back communist imperialism," or a *pax sovietica* that some Western commentators, taking note of the relative decline in United States military strength vis-à-vis the Soviet Union, have come to fear — are not realistic in terms of the new balance of political forces in the world community in the last part of the century. The United States Government discovered to its cost, in the Vietnam conflict, that it no longer had either the military-technological capacity or the necessary popular backing to maintain a Victorian, "policeman of the world" rôle. Any Soviet dreams of undivided world hegemony also disappeared with the shattering of the myth that the communist world would always act as one when the Chinese leaders broke with Soviet leadership and decided to go their own way in 1959. The complexity of post-détente political currents in the world community has meant that the two big powers have increasingly been cast in defensive rôles where they are unable to profit from evident, supervening weakness in the other side's position. The best example of this was the traumatic American withdrawal from Vietnam after the military defeat of the American "client government" in Saigon and the downfall of the Nixon strong (or "imperial") presidency at home. Not only was the Soviet Union unable to fill the vacuum left by the American departure and extend its own influence in South East Asia, but a natural balance immediately emerged, in the region, between Soviet and Chinese power. This development discredited, retroactively, the whole "falling dominoes" axiom — that the fall of any one country would automatically mean the fall of its neighbours, one after another — on which the disastrous American intervention in South Vietnam had been based in the first place. Likewise, the United States Government's assorted ills in Iran at the end of the 1970s after the downfall of the Shah's régime — historically traceable to the equally ill-advised, American CIA-backed military overthrow of the Mossadeq Government and the imposed restoration of the Shah in 1953 — did not automatically open the way to a Soviet takeover. Soviet political involvement in neighbouring Afghanistan, beginning several years before with the installation of the first of several pro-Soviet, Afghan Governments, was spotlighted by the clumsiness and heavy-handedness of the direct military takeover in early 1980. This incident indicated the effective limits and restraints on Soviet power, even in dealing with tiny neighbours on its own doorstep. The Soviet Union would have risked far greater outside opposition, from the Islamic world much more than the West, by entering upon any larger Iranian "adventure" taking advantage of American weakness in that country.

The period of transition we now live in, reflecting the world revolution of our times, has implications not merely for the basis of world public order — the political-military and economic facts of life on which relations between states are predicated — but also in the general realm of ideas and goal values to be pursued by the world community, or its dominant coalition of political-ideological forces, in shaping community decision making. If the present era of transition has meant a plurality of effective participants in community decision making in place of the big power condominium of yesterday, it has also meant a plurality of voices as to the right solution for any one problem-situation. An age of transition is only rarely an age of consensus on the direction of the new society that is emerging in place of the old. This places special strains upon decision makers, national and international. The international lawyer who is so often, today, the actual political decision maker or at least the *éminence grise* standing behind him, tends to take an élitist position and assume that the international decision-making process can be reduced to a scientific exercise: the conscious adducing and weighing of social and economic facts, followed by rational choice among the alternative policy options revealed by that empirical inquiry. Law, on this view, becomes the handmaiden of society, and legal decision makers respond directly to the objective, scientific and technological *données* of the world community of our times.

To speak of science and technology together with international law is to imply a more or less inevitable relation between general scientific and technological change, and international legal change. Dicey, in his rightly celebrated *Law and Opinion in England*, and the continental European and North American schools of sociological jurisprudence in general, tended to preach the symbiosis between law and society in an historically determinist way. They implied not merely that there ought to be a conscious and continuing attempt by decision makers to relate positive law to changing societal needs and expectations, but that basic social facts automatically controlled the positive law in the sense that any legal system, to be effective and therefore deserve the name of law, could not run too far in advance of, or more importantly lag too far behind, the society it claimed to represent.

Sociological jurisprudence, as developed variously by continental European jurists like von Ihering, Stammler, Duguit, and Durkheim, and by Dean Roscoe Pound in North America, basically connoted legal relativism. The test of "goodness" in law was the extent to which it gave effect to the aspirations of the main contending groups in society, who were themselves, of course, reacting to the fundamental facts of life of the world around them. These community facts included physical and environmental facts like the availability and variety of food supplies; biological facts like population growth, and its relation to food and other natural resources; industrialization, and its effect upon the traditional family and other forms of social organization; and, not least, psychological facts, among which the reactions of individuals and social groups to rapid industrialization and urbanization figured very largely.

The impact of strictly scientific thinkers upon legal theory, at a time when the sociological schools of law were becoming dominant — in the late nineteenth and early twentieth centuries in continental Europe and the first half of the twentieth century in North America — was considerable, even if not all-pervasive. Scientists like Darwin, teaching their theories of the life struggle and the process of natural selection, strongly influenced the "social statics" of Herbert Spencer, while Malthus's views on the relation of fixed food supplies to a proliferating world population were known to, and influenced, legal as well as political thinkers throughout the nineteenth century. Beyond that, Comte's scientific positivism, in its deliberate rejection of metaphysics in favour of rigorously empirical methods, argued that nature must be viewed objectively in a value-neutral, non-ideological way. Implicit in Comte's approach, however, was an apparent assumption of the inevitability of human progress through the use of new scientific knowledge as well as a further, and far less warranted assumption, that such scientific empiricism is itself free from metaphysical elements and hidden value judgements.

The failure of the natural sciences to have a more decisive or pervasive influence on legal theory and legal development, in spite of nineteenth-century optimism that mankind would learn to master natural forces and turn them to the general welfare, is due to several factors. Only one of these is the absence of substantial scientific sophistication on the part of jurists and the political decision makers whom they counselled. The more important explanations lie in the relative lack of development in the natural sciences themselves, and in natural scientists' own comprehension of their scientific facts, to the point where those scientific facts could begin to shape, and really control, political decision making. The Malthusian theories, for example — based on the socially frightening hypothesis that human population multiplied according to a geometric progression, whereas food production increased on the basis of an arithmetic progression only — were largely vitiated, in their logical implications for political and social decision makers, by radical improvements in agricultural yield (through the rationalization of agricultural production), and by the development of new sources of food through the nineteenth-century European wave of colonial development overseas. Any other similarly reasoned scientific theses concerning finiteness of natural resources and the non-finite demands of a rapidly growing human population were largely disposed of by late nineteenth- and early twentieth-century patterns of state decision making. These included recourse to political or economic colonialism as a means of supplementing one's own scarce natural resources, or recourse to war against one's economically more richly-endowed, but militarily weaker neighbors. The German political drive for *Lebensraum* in the 1930s was, after all, an exercise of one policy option among the several policy options presumably available to correct the deficiencies in basic mineral resources and agricultural production in the highly-industrialized rump German state of the post-Versailles Treaty era, just as the accompanying German government-sponsored racist theories can be viewed as an application, albeit a highly perverted application, of social Darwinism and theories of natural selection. Imperial Japan's military expansionist drive to establish its own South East Asia "co-prosperity sphere" was simply another application of the same basic thesis, though without quite the same pathologically racist undertones.

To recall Hitler and imperial Japan is, of course, to remind ourselves that natural scientists, as participants in the process of social decision making, did not enjoy a particularly favourable public image in the immediate post-World War II years. There was a tendency to link scientists to outrages perpetrated by Germany and Japan, in whose service they had so ably and efficiently marshalled all the instruments of advanced scientific and technological knowledge. Yet the massive scientific and technological advances achieved in World War II and afterwards, especially in the area of nuclear power and nuclear weapon technology, have clearly changed some of the basic societal elements or *données* that have militated against the full utilization of scientific teachings in social decision making. The alternative option so frequently available to a national decision maker in past years, when his technical and economic advisers reported that the state was about to exhaust its natural resources in any area — namely, recourse to war, something vainly sought to be excluded from the range of legally permissible options by the ill-fated Kellogg-Briand Pact of 1928 — is presumably now excluded as a rational political option, at least in the case of big power conflict, because of the consequences of military-nuclear power when applied, as it surely would be, on a retaliatory basis.

For other situations, where no big power interests are directly involved or where those interests are peripheral at best, the process of world community decision making inevitably becomes much more complex and diffuse, without the concrete direction flowing from active big power leadership. The process of community decision making, in such cases, would ideally follow the UN Charter-envisaged procedures, leading to an ultimately universal consensus obtained through discussion in the UN General Assembly or in UN-sponsored international technical conferences. However, recent world community experience shows that the process in such cases is likely to be somewhat more anarchic, involving a plethora of unilaterally-asserted national claims and counterclaims that correspond more or less nakedly to national special interests, with only a token attempt to reconcile those individual national claims with more comprehensive world community perspectives.

The really persuasive demonstrations of the power of scientific and technological facts, by themselves, to produce rational decisions (given only ordinary common sense and humanity on the part of the national decision makers involved) are, as a matter of record, drawn from essentially big power, bipolar, political-military configurations where the mutual interests of the two major participants have been clear. Not so clear and inevitable, however, is the result in polypolar or multipolar situations where the number and range of participants militate against both substantial decision-making consensus, and minimum agreement on the range of scientific and technological facts upon which rational decision making must be predicated. Some examples will illustrate the basic decision-making dilemmas faced by the contemporary, pluralistic world community.

Countries like the United States, under pressure from populist, environmental protection lobbies, have actively applied bans or similar, crippling, administrative restrictions on overflights and landings of the newly developed, supersonic, civil passenger transport aircraft. These particular countries, in support of their regulation of international civil air transportation, have tended to maximize the importance of scientific data demonstrating the long-range dangers to the terrestrial atmosphere from such supersonic aircraft. On the other hand, countries like France and the Soviet Union, which pressed ahead with the commercial manufacture of such aircraft in the interests of national exports, have tended to play down any such hazards, to maximize the positive contributions of the aircraft to the development of international communications, and to promote, in that special sense at least, the international law principle of "freedom of the air."

With respect to the problem of birth control, diametrically opposing conclusions are likely to be reached in the world community, not merely on the range of possible community solutions, but even on the underlying societal facts and thus on the very definition of the problem itself. Contemporary neo-Malthusians point with alarm to the rapid growth of world population and to the comparative lag in the development of new food supplies, and reach the more or less inevitable conclusion that an effective agreement on world population control is one of the main imperatives of international law in the last part of the century — perhaps the number one priority as the risk of all-out nuclear war between the two superpowers recedes, with the attainment of a reciprocal, nuclear stalemate and concomitant (Soviet-Western) détente. Yet one can hardly avoid noticing that almost all of the main spokesmen on this behalf are from fully developed, highly industrialized countries with relatively static population growth rates. The achievement by Japan, as a non-white country, of internal national consensus on a levelling-off of population growth at 100 million people; the valiant efforts of Madame Gandhi's government in India to encourage restraint in population growth (sometimes by methods that may have offended "received," Western, constitutional-libertarian notions); the interest by the post-"Gang of Four" government of the People's Republic of China in containing the Chinese population at its present level, in the recognition that burgeoning numbers after the liberation war of the 1940s tended to cancel out the enormous social and economic gains made by the agrarian and industrial revolutions of the 1950s and 1960s — all these stand out as special examples of rational acts of national decision making by intellectually very courageous and well-endowed national political élites responding to the imperatives, as they saw them, of objective societal facts (food supplies, living space, the balance between industrial growth and traditional lifestyle, the physical and economic limits to community social and welfare services). It is, however, only too evident that many of the developing countries still see a political advantage in their very numbers, in the absence of more affirmative, or economically more realizable, assets. In any case, the developing countries as a whole do not seem to view the issue of the population-food balance with quite the same urgency as the developed countries. How do we reach international agreement under these circumstances, and what sort of effective international agreement can reasonably be expected to go beyond the publicizing and encouragement of purely voluntary measures?

To take another major problem area, we may at first agree that everyone is opposed to marine pollution, and that everyone is therefore in favour of international legal control of such a risk. Yet the unhappy history of the attempts to regulate marine pollution by legal means, suggests that the ship-owning countries operating large tanker fleets, and the major oil-importing countries to whose defence and other security or industrial needs a free flow of oil is vital, will join together and effectively moderate any proposed controls on oil pollution at sea that are likely to impose extra economic or other burdens upon marine transport of oil — in terms of either costly additional security and strengthening devices on the tankers themselves, or time-consuming restrictions on the navigational course and marine passage followed by those tankers. The interests of states having large coastlines and no large tanker fleets are of course clear, and their pressures for an international convention with stern enforcement measures are perfectly understandable in this light. In the absence of a genuine international consensus in the world community to date, either as to the exact nature of the problem revealed by the scientific facts, or as to the most appropriate control measures, we are likely to be left with the anarchy of individual national attempts at control measures on a purely unilateral basis. There is a strong suspicion, as in the case of the Arctic Waters Pollution Control measures proclaimed by Canada in 1970, that the control measures may be designed to promote covertly other, national economic interests at the same time as the announced pollution control objective.

When we reach the area of general protection of the environment, we once more come up against the fact that the price of absolute protection against environmental damage caused by industrialization, may be the economic and social benefits of living in an advanced industrial society. It is not surprising, in this light, that for certain of the "developing" countries of Africa, Asia, and Latin America, and even for certain already developed but still capital-importing countries, it may be considered worthwhile to play down the preservation of an ecological balance, lest the fear of overly stringent governmental controls drive away much-needed foreign investment. Stringent controls may seem to be a luxury that only the highly industrialized and capital-rich countries can currently afford. In this regard, there would seem to be a need for more research and public education into the possibilities of usefully combining environmental protection with industrial development, without adding unduly to the cost factor for developing countries. Perhaps, in addition, a special United Nations-administered capital fund with required minimum contributions by the post-industrial societies could ease, and ideally eliminate, economic losses to developing countries that attempt to protect an existing natural environment.

All this simply confirms the truth that, while scientific and technological facts are an indispensable aid to rational community decision making, those facts will not necessarily be identified and appraised by national decision makers in quite the same way — except for countries at approximately the same level of social and economic development, with the same relative degree of scientific and technological sophistication. As yet, it is hardly likely that we will see general acceptance of any one, universally valid "truth" in a particular area of scientific inquiry, or general consensus on any one, scientifically valid community solution flowing logically from the "facts" of that inquiry. Instead, the process of community decision making is likely to involve the same balancing of competing national interests that we see in any area of international decision making; the interests concerned will cover, with varying degrees of national emphasis, the whole spectrum of military-strategic, ethno-cultural, economic, and other considerations that are invariably involved in decision making. The additional factor today, perhaps, is that the natural scientist speaks with renewed public authority, in comparison with the military commander, the political nationalist, or the industrial manager. When the natural scientist uses that prestige to make recommendations for control measures affecting the survival of mankind he can — as the examples of the Antarctic Treaty of 1959, the Moscow Partial Test Ban Treaty of 1963, and related disarmament measures show — sometimes summon heavy battalions to his aid that outweigh those of more conventional government advisers.

Among the key legal antinomies of the present era we can identify the following ones, conditioned in their application by either of the two main developmental constructs that we have already established as to the transition from a big power-dominated and effectively regulated world community, to a more genuinely pluralistic one in which more and more states, in more and more regional groupings, will come to participate in effective decision making in more and more problem areas. Some states will participate in most decisions in most areas; others will be limited, by the facts of physical power or of their own economic or ethno-cultural particularity, to a few decisions in only a few special areas.

First, with the evident decline in the spirit of big power

détente and in its actual use in Soviet-US conflict resolution and cooperation, and with pressures from the third world for a consequent "internationalizing" of both the participants and processes of international problem solving, will we see a return of effective international law decision-making power to the United Nations and its main specialized agencies, in accordance with the original intentions of the Charter and the first decade of practice thereunder, but with a new third world coalition dominating the United Nations in place of the former, pro-Western voting majority? Will this mean, inevitably, a successful challenge to the postwar emphasis upon East-West, big power Summit Meetings and direct, bilateral negotiation between the different blocs as the prime mode of international problem solving and conflict resolution? The antinomies, here, are between the limited, bilateral technique, and the multilateral, more nearly universal one; and between the informal, unstructured approach, and an institutionalized one that emphasizes the organized community decision-making arenas of the United Nations.

Second, speaking in international institutional terms, the years since the landmark decision rendered by an 8 to 7 vote in 1966 in the *South West Africa* case, have seen a movement away from the International Court of Justice and from judicial settlement of international conflicts generally. On the one hand, third world countries view the Court, and the judicial process as applied to international problem solving, as politically loaded in favour of the status quo and a species of "white man's" law. On the other hand, older post-industrial societies — both Western and Soviet but for quite different substantive reasons — are also reacting to a certain "politicization" that they see emerging in the Court's work. The Western countries now prefer to settle their own disputes *inter partes* through special arbitral tribunals limited to their own members; the Soviet bloc opts instead for direct diplomatic negotiation and related means. Will the increasing politicization of the election of judges bring a more intellectually activist, third world-leaning, judicial majority on the Court, and thus encourage a conscious resort to the Court for the creation of a "new" international law through judicial legislation? If so, any expansion in Court business will hardly come via the contentious jurisdiction route, since that depends, ultimately, on the consent of states, but via the Advisory Opinion route, which rests on the initiative of the UN General Assembly Secretary-General. The basic antinomy, in any case, is between the judicial settlement of disputes — once so highly favoured by Western jurists and foreign ministries in the days of Western political ascendancy in the old League of Nations and the early United Nations — and other modes of dispute settlement favouring diplomatic and more consciously political methods.

Third, will all the pressures by the third world for the creation of a new international economic order by legislative *fiat* of the UN General Assembly — the Declaration on the Establishment of a New International Economic Order, the Programme of Action, and the further Charter of Economic Rights and Duties of States — be successful, or will it be resisted by those post-industrial societies whose cooperation seems necessary to the active implementation of that ideal in the immediate future? I am not sure if one can, in the foreseeable future, expect to replace a political-military base for world public order by a predominantly economic one, though Professor Schwarzenberger has reminded us of an earlier, fundamentally economically-based system, the so-called *Pax Britannica*, which in his words . . . "rested on the combined might of the City of London and the British Navy. In the last resort needy governments and private entrepreneurs had to take their cue from the City of London on what would-be 'host' countries expected of the borrowers."

Both the objective of a new, economic base for world public order and, perhaps, the ultimate ideal of a world "rule of law" and the logically-formal rationality of a classical, juridically-based system, rest on the solution of pressing and hitherto irreconcilable political conflicts and the development of a new, more genuinely pluralistic consensus in the world community that will replace the old emphasis on political-military power relationships. The basic antinomy, here, is between a new economic base for ordering international relations, and the older, political-military base. The further, conjoined antimony is between a world economic system that emphasizes the sharing of resources and the approach to equalization of economic riches between different states, and the more orthodox patterns of world banking and trade that have been dominant up to this point.

Fourth, will the movement to internationalize the "common heritage of all mankind" — the seabed, the ocean floor, and their economic resources — succeed and be extended? Or will we see a continuance and extension of the principle, supposedly derived from classical international law, that they are open to all comers (meaning, in contemporary terms, only the technologically advanced societies, both Soviet and western)? The antimony here is an easier one to discern, for it is between a larger pooling of world resources without regard to one's industrial base or economic development, and more classical entrepreneurial theories of "finders as keepers."

Fifth, will the principle of self-determination of peoples continue to grow and to be applied, notwithstanding the near completion of the historical process of decolonization (European-style) with which it has always been linked in the post-World War II period? Or will it yield to countervailing international law principles, such as the principle of the integrity of territorial frontiers? In post-colonial Africa, for example, those frontiers may have been inherited from the parent, European colonial power. In strict international law terms, the antinomy is between self-determination of peoples, and non-intervention in the internal affairs of another state (here, the integrity of its inherited territorial frontiers). In larger policy terms, the antinomy is often between elemental peace keeping in politically very fragile, former colonies in Africa and Asia, and full allegiance to one of the "new" international law's imperative principles or *jus cogens*, so imaginatively and persuasively extended in the post-World War II fight for decolonization and independence.

Sixth, will the principle of non-intervention in the internal, domestic affairs of a state prevail over "new" international law claims for the internationalization of what was previously considered national — namely, national action or inaction, at the municipal law level, in regard to ethno-cultural or religious minorities within the existing nation-state? The implications of the new "humanitarian international law," argued by some Western leaders to be implicit in such recent international law-making ventures as the Helsinki Final Act, are clear — not only for big power détente, but also long-range for the whole concept of domestic jurisdiction as traditionally construed. Once one opens the door to a discussion of the domestic policies of particular states, as proper subjects of international concern, it is hardly possible to limit the discussion to purely Western-based concepts of human rights. Western legal systems have tended to stress individual rights, the most important of these being political rights. Other legal systems prefer to emphasize collective or group rights, the most important of these being economic rights, including "new" rights like the right to work, or to be guaranteed minimum standards of living, or to be guaranteed minimum sharing in the riches of society. Further, every juridical right implies a correlative legal duty. A postulated political right to emigrate from any one state means, logically, a correlative legal duty of other states to receive the "political" émigré. From there, it may be only a legal hop-skip-and-a-jump to a "new" international law-based duty of states to receive "economic" refugees (the world's poor, fleeing their own inhospitable home country to other, richer states), or to a further duty on the part of richer countries that also happen to be thinly populated to open their frontiers to United Nations-based projects for resettlement of the poor. The strict legal antinomy here is between the Charter principle of non-intervention in the internal affairs of states, and the "new" principle of the internationalization of human rights. The larger, policy antinomy is between a state's control of its own human resources, including decisions on whom it lets out and whom it admits or rejects, and a postulated world community interest in solving world population growth problems through planned resettlement and redirection programmes.

Finally, and adverting now to Radbruch's basic example — the antinomy between stability and change in law itself — will the present attempts to modernize classical international law doctrine, in accordance with changing societal demands and expectations in the world community, by using existing international institutions and existing international law techniques (multilateral or bilateral treaties, judicial interpretations, developing custom and convention) yield significant incremental change? Or will we see, instead, the continued and extended use of extra-legal means — direct action, including political terrorism — as instruments of social change in a rapidly evolving world community? The escalation of civic violence as a means of legal change — in both national and international contexts — and the evident inability of public order systems effectively to counter it, are among the most striking phenomena of the law and society relation of our times. The two superpowers, in their mutually developed, inter-bloc "rules of the game," treat terrorism and other forms of direct action (including espionage, and the use of diplomatic premises for the subversion of the "host" or receiving government) easily and elegantly, on an *inter partes* basis. In relationships where an effective power imbalance exists, however — such as those between post-industrial societies on the one hand, and developing, third world countries on the other — reciprocal self-interest is hardly available as a weapon of social control. In such situations direct action, with all the gratuitous violence to innocent people that it so often entails, becomes the outlet for social frustration, bringing a breakdown in friendly relations among states and an invitation to ever-escalating direct action by way of reprisal. The urgency of the challenge to bridge-building — between the first and second worlds on the one hand, and the emerging third world countries on the other — becomes apparent, as does the need to construct a more equitable, and more genuinely inclusive, world economic and public order system.

Table of Cases

1 *Status of Eastern Carelia*, Advisory Opinion of 23 July 1923, P.C.I.J. Series B, No. 5, p. 7.
2 *Conditions of Admission of a State to Membership in the United Nations*, Advisory Opinion of 28 May 1948, I.C.J. Reports 1948, p. 57.
3 *Certain Expenses of the United Nations*, Advisory Opinion of 20 July 1962, I.C.J. Reports 1962, p. 151.
4 *South West Africa, Preliminary Objections*, Judgment, I.C.J. Reports 1962, p. 319.
5 *South West Africa, Second Phase*, Judgment, I.C.J. Reports 1966, p. 6.
6 *North Sea Continental Shelf*, Judgment, I.C.J. Reports 1969, p. 3.
7 *Legal Consequences for States of the Continued Presence of South Africa in Namibia (South West Africa) Notwithstanding Security Council Resolution 276 (1970)*, Advisory Opinion, I.C.J. Reports 1971, p. 16.
8 *Nuclear Tests, (Australia v. France), Interim Protection*, Order of 22 June 1973, I.C.J. Reports 1973, p. 99.
9 *Nuclear Tests, (Australia v. France)*, Judgment of 20 December 1974, I.C.J. Reports 1974, p. 253.
10 *Western Sahara*, Advisory Opinion, I.C.J. Reports 1975, p. 12.
11 *United States Diplomatic and Consular Staff in Tehran, Provisional Measures*, Order of 15 December 1979, I.C.J. Reports 1979, p. 7.
12 *United States Diplomatic and Consular Staff in Tehran, (United States of America v. Iran)*, Judgment of 24 May 1980, I.C.J. Reports 1980.

Selected Bibliography

Acheson, Dean. *Power and Diplomacy.* 1958.
Agrawala, S.K. *Aircraft Hijacking and International Law.* 1973.
───────. *Essays on the Law of Treaties.* 1972.
Alvarez, A. *Le Droit International Nouveau dans ses rapports avec la Vie actuelle des Peuples.* 1959.
Anand, R.P. *Studies in International Adjudication.* 1969.
Andrassy, J. "Les relations internationales de voisinage." 79 Recueil des Cours (Académie de la Haye) 77 (1951).
Arangio-Ruiz, G. "The normative rôle of the General Assembly of the United Nations and the Declaration of Principles of Friendly Relations." Recueil des Cours 419 (1972).
Asamoah, O. *The Legal significance of the Declarations of the General Assembly of the United Nations.* 1966.
Bedjaoui, M. "Non-alignement et droit international." 151 Recueil des Cours 337 (1976).
───────. *Pour un nouvel ordre économique international.* 1979.
───────. *Terra nullius, "droits" historiques et auto-détermination.* 1975.
Blegvad, M. et al., eds. *Festskrift til Professor Alf Ross.* 1969.
Bloomfield, L.M. and FitzGerald, G.F. *Crimes against Internationally Protected Persons: Prevention and Punishment.* 1975.
Brandt, Willy, ed. *North-South: A Programme for Survival..* 1980.
Brownlie, Ian. *International Law and the Use of Force by States.* 1963.
Brucan, S. *The Dialectic of World Politics.* 1978.
Calogeropoulos-Stratis, S. *Le droit des peuples à disposer d'eux-mêmes.* 1973.
De Visscher, C. *Théories et réalités en droit international public.* 1955.
Dupuy, René-Jean. *The Law of the Sea. Current Problems.* 1974.
Elias, T.O. *New Horizons in International Law.* 1979.

Falk, R. et al., eds. *The Strategy of World Order. International Law.* 1966.
Friedmann, W. *The Changing Structure of International Law.* 1964.
Gardner, Richard N. *In Pursuit of World Order.* 1964.
Goodrich, L.M. and Hambro, E. *Charter of the United Nations. Commentary and Documents.* 2d rev. ed. 1949.
Gross, Leo, "The International Court of Justice and the United Nations." *Recueil des Cours* 313 (1967).
Grzybowski, K. *Soviet Public International Law. Doctrines and Diplomatic Practice.* 1970.
Hazard, John N. "Codifying Peaceful Coexistence." 55 *American Journal of International Law* 109 (1961).
Jenks, C. Wilfred. *The Common Law of Mankind.* 1958.
Jiménez de Aréchaga, E. *Derecho Constitucional de las Naciones Unidas.* 1958.
_____. "International Law in the past Third of a Century." *Recueil des Cours* 1 (1978).
Kozhevnikov, F.I., ed. *International Law. A Textbook for Use in Law Schools.* 1962.
Krause-Ablass, W.-D. *Intertemporales Völkerrecht.* 1970.
Kulski, W.W. *Peaceful Coexistence.* 1959.
Lachs, M. *The Law of Outer Space. An Experience in Contemporary Law-Making.* 1972.
Lasswell, H.D. *The World Revolution of Our Time. A Framework for Basic Policy Research.* 1951.
Lauterpacht, Sir H. *The Development of International Law by the International Court.* 1958.
McDougal, M.S. "International Law, Power and Policy: A Contemporary Conception." 82 *Recueil des Cours* 140 (1953).
McDougal, M.S. and Feliciano, F.P. *Law and Minimum World Public Order. The Legal Regulation of International Coercion.* 1961.
McDougal. M.S. et al. *Studies in World Public Order.* 1960.
McNair, Lord. *The Law of Treaties.* 1961.
McWhinney, Edward. *Conflit idéologique et Ordre public mondial.* 1970.
_____ *The Illegal Diversion of Aircraft and International Law.* 1975.
_____. *The International Law of Détente. Arms Control, European Security, and East-West Cooperation.* 1978.
_____. *The World Court and the Contemporary International Lawmaking Process.* 1979.
Morgenthau, Hans J. *Politics among Nations.* 2d rev. ed. 1954.
Mosler, H. and Bernhardt, R., eds. *Judicial Settlement of International Disputes.* 1974.

Mosler, H. "The International Society as Legal Community." *Recueil des Cours* 1 (1974).
Nawaz, M.K., ed. *Essays on International Law in honour of Krishna Rao.* 1975.
Oda, Shigeru. *The Law of the Sea in our Time.* 1977.
Panzera, A.F. *Attività terroristiche e Diritto internazionale.* 1978.
Parry, Clive. *The Sources and Evidences of International Law.* 1965.
Radbruch, Gustav. *Rechtsphilosophie.* 4th ed. 1950.
Röling, B.V.A. *International Law in an Expanded World.* 1960.
Rosenne, S. *The International Court of Justice.* 1961.
_____. *The Law of Treaties.* 1970.
Ross, Alf. *The United Nations. Peace and Progress.* 1966.
Schwarzenberger, Georg. "An Evolving Economic World Order." 1 *Rutgers-Camden Law Journal* 243 (1969).
Sepulveda, Cesar. *Curso de Derecho Internacional Publico.* 2d ed. 1964.
Sorensen, Max, ed. *Manual of Public International Law.* 1968.
Stone, Julius. *Aggression and World Order. A critique of United Nations Theories of Aggression.* 1958.
_____. *Conflict through Consensus, United Nations Approaches to Aggression.* 1977.
_____. *Legal Controls of International Conflict.* 1954.
Tunkin, G.I. *Droit International Public. Problèmes théoriques.* 1965.
_____. *Theory of International Law.* 1974.
_____. *Teoria mezhdunarodnogo prava.* 1970.
Wilkinson, Paul. *Terrorism and the Liberal State.* 1977.
Willrich, Mason. *Non-Proliferation Treaty: Framework for Nuclear Arms Control.* 1969.
Willrich, Mason and Rhinelander, J.B., eds. *SALT. The Moscow Agreements and Beyond.* 1974.

Index

Advisory opinions, 61-62, 64, 65, 67, 149
Afghanistan, 141
Aggression, legal definition, 91-92
Ammoun, Judge, 26-27, 66, 67
Antinomies, legal, 117, 127, 139, 148-153
Apartheid, 59, 61, 128

Bedjaoui, M., 19, 66
Bilateral treaties, 20, 30-31, 77, 83, 85, 132, 152
Bipolarity, Soviet-US, 16, 19, 29, 41, 43, 57, 93, 97, 137, 140
Boni, ad hoc Judge, 66, 67
Brandt, Chancellor, 77, 136
"Brezhnev Doctrine," 93
Brezhnev, L., 79, 87
Bystricky, R., 121

Carter, President, 88, 122
Charter, UN, 36, 37, 38, 39, 40, 41, 42, 44, 45, 46, 48, 50, 53, 54-57, 62, 76, 85, 92, 100, 108, 135, 144, 149
Chayes, A., 35
China, People's Republic of, 43, 73, 74, 82, 83, 118, 146
Civil Aviation Organization, International, 124
Codification, legal, 96, 131, 132
Cold war, 15, 20, 33, 34, 42, 43, 45, 56, 57, 69, 73, 74, 93, 97, 98, 102, 115, 119, 137, 138
Colonialism, 14, 26, 50, 51, 65, 66, 74, 128, 133, 143
Continental shelf, 23, 131, 132
Court, World, 25-27, 32, 41, 53-55, 57-65, 67-70, 112, 118, 123, 149
Cuba, missile crisis, 16, 28, 30, 32-37, 45, 84, 92, 97
Czechoslovakia, 93

Decade of Development, UN, 119, 121
Decolonisation, 14, 15, 17, 24, 65, 72, 116, 132, 133, 134, 135, 136, 151
de Gaulle, President, 82, 119, 137
Détente, Soviet-US, 16, 19, 32, 37-38, 71-79, 84-85, 88, 89, 91, 93-94, 98, 99, 104, 107, 109, 110, 111, 116-118, 121, 122, 132, 137-140, 146, 148-149, 151
Domestic jurisdiction, 67, 151
"Dominoes, falling," 141

Economic order, new international, 18, 19, 23, 24, 118, 123, 126, 133, 135, 136, 150
Economic Rights and Duties of States, Charter of, 18, 127-129, 150
Expenses, UN, Advisory Opinion, 49-50, 53, 54, 55

Fitzmaurice, Judge, 63
Ford, President, 87
Forster, Judge, 27, 66, 67
Friendly Relations, UN Declaration of, 96, 100-101
Frontiers, security of, 15, 38, 71-72, 73, 76-77, 89, 117, 151

General Assembly, UN, 18, 26, 29, 31, 37-38, 39-52, 82, 83, 91, 92, 95-96, 101, 105, 116, 119, 120, 121, 123, 125, 126, 127, 135, 136, 145, 150

Hammarskjöld, D., 49
Hegemony, big power, 16, 18, 82, 100, 118, 137
Helsinki, Declaration, 77-78, 89, 151
Humanitarian international law, 151
Hungary, 93, 97

International Monetary Fund, 109, 129
Iran, Shah of, 68, 70, 141
Iran, US v., judgement, 68-70

Jessop, Judge, 61
Johnson, President, 19, 84
Jus cogens, 70, 151

Kennedy, President, 30, 31, 32, 33, 34, 35, 36, 74, 84, 97, 98, 106, 107, 115, 119
Khrushchev, N.S., 30, 31, 33, 34, 36, 48, 72, 73, 74, 83, 84, 95, 96-97, 98, 106, 107, 115
Korean War, 17, 43, 44, 45, 56
Koretsky, Judge, 53, 54, 55, 59
Korovin, E., 25, 47, 114, 117
Kozhevnikov, Judge, 112
Krylov, Judge, 26, 39

Lachs, Judge, 26, 32, 51, 60, 69, 70, 104
"Little steps," politic of, 77, 89

159

McDougal, M.S., 112
McNair, Judge, 98
Mossadeq, Premier, 68, 141
Moscow Test Ban Treaty, 31-32, 81, 98, 103, 104, 106, 107, 148
Multilateral conventions, 126, 130-131, 135
Mutual Balanced Force Reductions, 89-91

Namibia (South West Africa), Advisory Opinion, 61-64, 67
"New" international law, 18, 19, 38, 72, 114, 149, 151-152
Nixon, President, 20, 141
Nixon-Brezhnev détente, 83, 85, 87, 107
Non-intervention, principle, 93-94, 97, 111, 151, 152
Non-Proliferation Treaty, 81-83
Nuclear disarmament, 38, 80-88, 89, 117
Nuclear Tests, judgement, 64-65

OPEC, 129, 130, 133, 136
Ostpolitik, 76-78, 89

Palestine Liberation Organization, 123, 124
Pashukanis, 117
Peaceful coexistence, principles, 85, 95-98, 99, 100, 116, 117, 121, 137
Piracy, aerial, 123-125
Polisario, 134
Potsdam Conference, 75, 138
Prebisch Gap, 119-120
Proliferation, nuclear, 19, 82

Radbruch, G., 139, 152
Resolutions, UN General Assembly, 18, 51-52, 106, 134
"Revisionism," 116

SALT I, 86
SALT II, 86, 87, 88, 91
Seabed, 83, 129, 132, 133, 151
Sea, Law of, UN Conference, 23, 122, 131-133
Secretary-General, UN, 31, 49, 105, 149
Security Council, UN, 26, 29, 39-52, 53, 56, 61, 62, 68, 92, 109, 125
Self-determination, principle, 14, 15, 63, 67, 72, 73, 74, 93, 116, 125, 135, 136, 138, 151
South West Africa, judgement, 58-61, 118, 149
Space, outer, 20, 104-107
Spender, Judge, 58, 59, 60
"Spheres of influence," 33, 93-94, 137
"Step by step" approach, 72, 81, 83, 84-85, 90, 98-99, 115
Stone, Julius, 92
Summit Meetings, 20, 31, 38, 47, 85, 87, 107

Terrorism, international, 122-126, 134, 152
"Third world," 18, 23, 24, 38, 46, 47, 60, 61, 64, 65, 72, 99, 100, 111, 118, 122-123, 125, 126, 127, 129, 130, 132, 133, 134, 135, 136, 139, 149, 150, 152-153
Tokyo Convention, 124
Tunkin, G.I., 47-48, 51-52, 98, 113-114, 116, 117

UNCTAD, 109, 119-121
"Uniting for Peace Resolution," 37, 44, 45, 46, 47, 51, 56

Vallat, Sir F., 114
Versailles, Treaty of, 21, 26, 40, 71, 91, 144
Veto, big power, 42, 43, 44, 46, 47, 48, 49, 50, 109
Vietnam War, 105, 122, 138, 140, 141

Weighted voting, UN, 109-110, 121
Western Sahara, Advisory Opinion, 26-27, 65-67, 134
Winiarski, Judge, 53, 54, 55, 59, 60

Yalta Conference, 26, 75, 138

Date Due

FEB 23 '90			
FEB 03 '93			
MAR 05 '93			
MAR 19 '93			
JAN 19 '96			

BRODART, INC.   Cat. No. 23 233   Printed in U.S.A.